For my brother Paul Halas whose memories of our mother may be different to mine, his sons Danny, Joe and Oliver and my daughter Sophie.

Special thanks to
Mike Swift who designed and produced this book, and the support of all the contributors including Brian Sibley, Jez Stewart, Clare Kitson, Jim Walker, Paul Wells and Peter Lord, and interviewees, Vera Linnecar, Stella Harvey, Christine Jollant, Monique Renault, Bridget Heal, Geoff and Linda Halpin, Richard Oliver and Paul Halas.

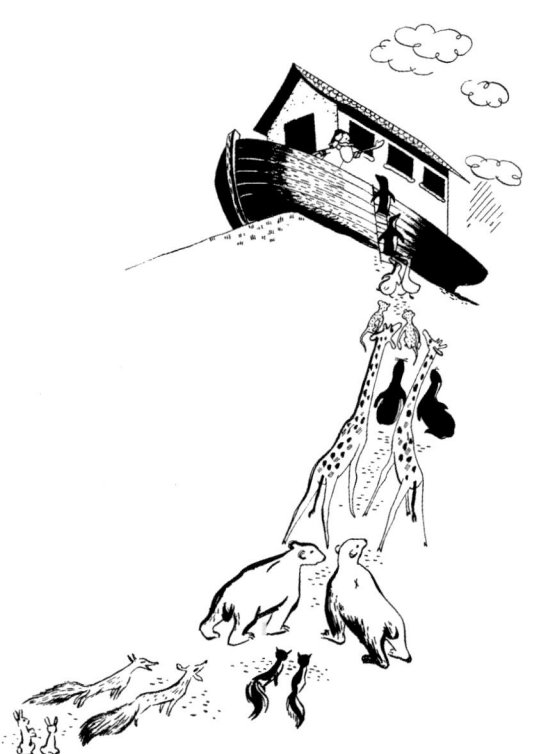

First edition published in 2014 by Southbank Publishing
21 Great Ormond Street, London WC1N 3JB
www.southbankpublishing.com

© The Halas & Batchelor Collection Limited 2014

The right of Vivien Halas to be identified as author of this work has been asserted in accordance with the Copyright, Designs and Patents Act 1988.

All rights reserved. No part of this book may be reproduced, stored in or introduced into a retrieval system, or transmitted, in any form or by any means (electronic, mechanical, photocopying, recording or otherwise) without the written permission of the publisher.

Any person who does any unauthorised act in relation to this publication may be liable to criminal prosecution and civil claims for damages.

A CIP catalogue for this book is available from the British Library.

ISBN 978-1-904915-41-6

Book design by Mike Swift.

All photographs and illustrations courtesy of The Halas & Batchelor Collection unless otherwise stated.

A moving image
Joy Batchelor 1914-1991
Artist, writer and animator

Authors

Brian Sibley
Broadcaster, playwright, documentary presenter, critic and author of many books on film and animation including *Mickey Mouse: His Life and Times* (1986), *Snow White and the Seven Dwarfs: The Making of a Movie Classic* (1988) and *The Disney Studio Story* (1998), all co-authored with Richard Holliss; *Cracking Animation* (1998), co-authored with Peter Lord; *Chicken Run: Hatching the Movie* (2000), *The Lord of the Rings: The Making of the Movie Trilogy* (2002), *Peter Jackson: A Filmmaker's Journey* (2006), *Harry Potter Film Wizardry* (2010) and *The Making of 'The Pirates! In an Adventure with Scientists'* (2012).

Jez Stewart
Curator of non-fiction and animation with the British Film Institute National Archive responsible for the Halas & Batchelor archive. With a regular blog on the BFI website, he is also author of numerous articles on film and animation that explore British animation history from its beginnings.

Clare Kitson
Former commissioning editor for animation at Channel 4, and author of *British animation: The Channel 4 Factor* (2008) and *Yuri Norstein and the Tale of Tales* (2005), for which she learnt Russian, Clare is a regular member on international animation juries.

Vivien Halas
Daughter of Joy Batchelor and John Halas and a former graphic designer, she has directed the Halas & Batchelor Collection since 1996. She is co-author of *Halas & Batchelor cartoons: An Animated History* (2006) with Professor Paul Wells, and has contributed to numerous animation publications worldwide.

Jim Walker
Academic at the UCA, former manager of the Halas & Batchelor archive specialising in illustration, and author and curator of many festival programmes, the most recent being on the late Bob Godfrey. Author of *A Terror Lexicon: Shadows, Places and Ghosts in Art and the Age of Terrorism*, Graham Coulter Smith and Maurice Owen (2005).

Paul Wells
Director of the Animation Academy, Loughborough University, Professor Paul Wells has published widely in Animation Studies, including a collaboration with Vivien Halas: *Halas & Batchelor Cartoons: An Animated History*. He is an established screenwriter and director, recent documentaries include Geoff Dunbar, John Halas and Mackinnon & Saunders, and film scripts 'The Oil Kid' and 'Trios'. He also conducts workshops and consultancies worldwide based on his book *Scriptwriting* (2007).

Contents

3	**Ode to Joy**	*Brian Sibley*
7	**Artist, writer and animator**	*Jez Stewart*
23	**A woman's place**	*Clare Kitson*
31	**A personal memory**	*Vivien Halas*
41	**A gifted illustrator**	*Jim Walker*
59	**Joy, Britain needs you**	*Paul Wells*
80	**Filmography**	*Vivien Halas*
85	**Film selection**	

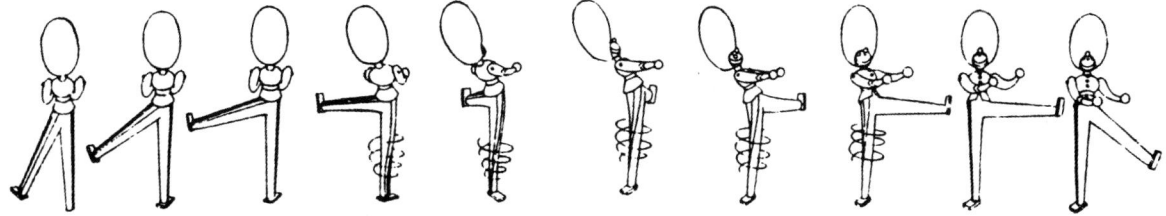

Ode to Joy *Brian Sibley*

'Hello,' I said, 'you must be Joy.' The year was 1980, the place London's Royal Festival Hall, the occasion the opening of an exhibition marking forty years of Halas & Batchelor. John, ever the showman, was, naturally, holding court, centre stage. I was interested, however, in meeting the co-founder of this famous studio whose work I had so long admired and where, a decade earlier, I had unsuccessfully tried to get a job.

We sat and chatted while John gave interviews and eventually made a speech that failed to mention Joy or her contributions to the success of the company and to British animation. To my astonishment, she seemed indifferent to being ignored, whereas I felt a sense of righteous indignation on her behalf.

That might have been my only contact with this amazingly creative woman, but the exhibition opening was followed by a celebratory meal and, as luck would have it, I was seated next to Joy.

The ice already having been broken, we were free to talk about animation, comparing the approaches of the American studios (and especially Disney) with that of Britain and Europe. We discussed the conflicting demands of art and commerce and talked, at some length, about *Animal Farm*, not just the film but also the illustrated edition of the book, published in 1954, in which - a rare event - Joy got first credit ahead of John!

Much has been written about the studio and its work over the years and, inevitably, it was either written *by* John, in collaboration *with* John or from a John-orientated perspective. A book focusing on the life and contribution of Joy is not only welcome but long overdue.

The role of women in the history and development of the art of animation has been crucial and yet, until relatively recently, largely ignored. True, the armies of 'ink and paint girls' were often acknowledged, though invariably in patronising tones, but it was always the male animators and directors who received the plaudits. Scandalously, this was even the case where female art directors and artists made an influential contribution to the design and animation of films.

Since Joy was frequently denied the on-screen credits to which she was entitled, some may question just how much she contributed to the creativity and development of the Halas & Batchelor studio. However, one has only to look at the examples of her art shown in the following pages to see her sense of style and the sureness of line that give her drawings (regardless of whether the subject is fanciful or prosaic) an exuberant vivacity. From her art school exercises, via her sketches for popular newspapers to her animation designs and those evocative illustrations to George Orwell's famous fable, the art of Joy Batchelor exhibits a knack for conveying personality and capturing the dynamism and immediacy of character and movement.

In addition to her artistry, her aptitude for storytelling and her considerable production skills, it is unquestionably the case that without Joy's aid, John might not have been so successful in the pursuit of his own talents. Additionally, of course, it was taken for granted by everyone (including John) that, at the same time, Joy would run a home and raise a family!

On several occasions, over the years, I interviewed John and wrote articles about him. I even penned a lyric for one of his films (uncredited of course!) so, having written about 'Halas', it gives me great pleasure to, at last, be able to contribute to the story of 'and Batchelor', the other, too-long-neglected, half of this great animation partnership.

Artist, writer and animator *Jez Stewart*

Joy Batchelor was born on May 12th, 1914, in a small terraced house in Watford, then a market town about twenty miles north of London. Craftsmanship ran through her recent ancestry: an artificer, a master cabinetmaker, and her father was a lithographic draughtsman. She described him as a gentle, quiet, kind and clever man, but with what she perceived as an over-cautious nature and a lack of ambition. His refusal to accept a position of management kept the aspirations of his family in check, frustrating any later ambition of Joy attending university, for example. She was the eldest of three children, but a younger brother died of diphtheria just two months after the arrival of her sister in 1921, which must have put a further strain on family life.

The desire to draw came early, and with a tireless dedication that she seemed to put into all her work in her early life. She credited her father with encouraging and developing her talent, bringing home shiny offcuts of quality paper from his work for her to use. She won a scholarship to grammar school, where she then gathered honours in French, History, Art and English. After a period at Watford School of Art, despite offers of further study, she had to find employment and start paying her way. Her career plans were vague - anything to do with art but teach, which was her parents' ambition for her.

Etching of the back garden of the family home, made by Joy while she was at Watford School of Art.

These images are from Joy's days at Watford Art School, where she was a star pupil. Her tutors wanted her to accept a place at the Slade but she had to decline because her parents, having supported her so far, needed her to contribute to the household. Joy is on the front row right.

At first this lead to a basic job painting ornaments and trinkets on an assembly line.

It is here that signs of her ambitious and adventurous drive became apparent. Not afraid to pass critical comment, even at a relatively tender age, she spoke out about the job and the working conditions and believes she was paid off for being a nuisance. Looking for a job in London she was offered a place at a new animation studio which was just being set up by a recently arrived Australian cartoonist, Dennis Connelly. She was initially hired at the start of 1934 as an inbetweener, creating the animation drawings that fell between the key frames set out by the higher-paid animators. But once again, she showed the assurance to speak out about the poor quality of the work, and this time was rewarded with a swift promotion to key animator.

The studio lasted barely three years, with very little achieved in that time, but before it closed Joy had a delightful taste of a modern, artistic, metropolitan life and was already earning more than her father. She had been bitten by the animation bug, and when the money ran out she looked for other work in the industry.
She was turned down by Hector Hoppin and Anthony Gross, who were making *Fox Hunt* (1936) with Alexander Korda as a follow up to

Images of cupids often crop up in Joy's illustrations, here in the film *The Fable of Fabrics* and in a book illustration from *The Truth about Stork* above.

their acclaimed *Joie De Vivre* (1934), and with little other work around she instead found a job designing posters.

Keen to escape the smell of silkscreen paint she spotted a small ad for a new animation studio, which was looking for experienced animators. She later said that her first thought was, 'Ah, this is your lucky day'. Not just for her, but also for her prospective new employer. She knew how few people in the country were qualified for such a job, and she was confident that she had real promise. That prospective employer was János Hálasz, recently arrived from his native Hungary and beginning to be known by his anglicised name, John Halas.

John's story has been told elsewhere, and it is hopefully sufficient to say here that his early, somewhat hand-to-mouth introduction to the animation industry had, by 1936, developed into running a successful studio in Budapest, with his partners Gyula Macskássy and Félix Kassowitz. When he was offered the chance to be the creative head of this new London enterprise, British Colour Cartoon Films Ltd, John jumped at the chance and cast around for animators, and that was how he came to meet Joy.

Writing in later life, Joy provided a fairly electric description of the moment they met: 'In addition to being an experienced animator I was not bad at exchanging looks. This one was riveting.' She also wrote, 'I think the attraction was instant and mutual, but work came first as it has done ever since. Shortly before the work on the film was finished we got together.' The film was *Music Man*, a film with some interesting designs filmed in Technicolor, but very variable quality. The film appears not have been shown in cinemas until 1938, where it swiftly disappeared. Joy was released after the film was completed and had to find other work, until John offered her the chance to make another film, back in Budapest.

Here then is an exciting, brave young woman, blossoming in her personal and creative life, and jumping into the great unknown of a distant European country. She spoke little to no Hungarian and was accompanied by a man who was both her lover and employer, and whose grasp of English was far from developed (she later wrote, 'we conversed through the media of pencil and paper, signs and gestures and some form of ESP. It worked pretty well.') Joy revelled in the experience and for the first time began to take a hand in the script and other pre-production roles, but the money ran out before the film was completed and they both returned to London to start again.

From 1937 to 1941 they ran a small graphic design studio off the Strand, advertising the services of 'Display. Posters. Folders. Fashion.' on their business card, working freelance on a huge variety of jobs and accounts, and building contacts that would come in immensely useful in the coming years. Vivien Halas has described their working relationship as follows: 'He had the vision and the Hungarian belief in his own excellence while Joy rewrote and translated what he did, not only into English, but, crucially, taking into account the British way of life. This is what gave them a unique edge to their work, the émigré energy combined with a sense of 'Britishness'.

Two factors seemed to have enabled their return to animation. Round the corner from their studio was the J Walter Thompson (JWT) advertising agency where Alexander Mackendrick was writing scripts and designing cinema publicity films - including a successful series of Horlicks adverts animated by George Pal in Holland. John had begun his animation career with George Pal back in Budapest, and Pal reportedly introduced them to JWT, before emigrating to Hollywood. When war broke out, paper shortages left advertisers with little space in newspapers for their advertisements, and as film stocks was not rationed, cinema advertising presented an attractive route to audiences. With George Pal's studio out of action, it must have seemed natural to bring the film-making experience of John and Joy onboard, and Halas & Batchelor Cartoon Films was born at Bush House under the wings of JWT.

For many years the company's first film was thought to have been *Train Trouble*, a five-minute cinema commercial for Kellogg's Cornflakes featuring what would be very accomplished design and animation for a first film. Work on the film may have begun at this time, but recent examination of the original film materials has suggested that it was certainly not completed before 1945 at the earliest, making *Carnival in the Clothes Cupboard* (c.1941) or *Fable of the Fabrics* (c.1942) the likeliest candidates. The latter film is a five-minute commercial for Lux washing powder, which reveals clear elements of the doe-eyes typical in Joy's character design of the period; a little cupid is a spitting image for her design for the baby in *Charley Junior's Schooldays* from 1949. There is also a dancing gypsy girl whose floating skirt is remarkably similar to the one that features in a test that Joy did for John when they first met.

In her freelancing design years Joy had done some work for Shell, liaising with their renowned publicity director Jack Beddington. In 1940 he was appointed as the head of the Ministry of Information's (MOI) film division, and Joy credited him with supplying them with a steady flow of work

Budapest
Joy and John were friends with Gyula Macskassy and his wife Vera. They took photos of each other in the street just below their studio on Rakóczi utca.

Lake Balaton
At weekends everyone went to Lake Balaton. Here is Joy at Balatonkenese at the northern end of the lake.

Publicity
This is one of a series of photos of Joy and John taken by Macskassy possibly to promote the studio.

Playing ping-pong
John and friends from the studio loved playing table tennis. These tournaments continued later in London during the war and remain one of the great memories of both Vera Linecar and Christine Jollant who worked both in Bush House and Soho Square.

Joy with rabbit
In the short time Joy lived in Budapest she took Hungarian lessons, worked hard, partied and had a pet angora rabbit.

Budapest studio
John, Joy and their business partners on the balcony overlooking Rakóczi utca.

View from the balcony
The building John and Joy worked in was destroyed during the war and exists today as a sad looking 1970s block housing a McDonalds. The Hotel Astoria next door gives more of an idea of how it was.

Bauhaus in Budapest
Between 1930 and 1948 there were many apartment blocks built in the Bauhaus style. John and Joy lived here at 99B.

Pasaréti utca in the 2nd district of Budapest, not far from their friend Gyogi Ranki the composer, who worked on *Brave Tin Soldier* (1938).

throughout the war. The first films, such as *Dustbin Parade* (1941) and *Filling the Gap* (1942), were made under the stewardship of the Realist Film Unit, assisted by documentary producer John Taylor. The studio quickly developed a successful style of melding anthropomorphic objects and cartoon physics into more realistically airbrushed textures and backgrounds. The scripts became increasingly skilled at presenting information with a direct yet accessible, non-patronising tone of voice.

The fact that Halas & Batchelor initially had to work through another unit may have been related to John's 'enemy alien' status, with his marriage to Joy on 26th April, 1940, apparently saving him from internment on the Isle of Man with so many other émigrés. Joy later wrote that they had previously held off marriage, thinking of it as an 'institution' which might 'wreck a good creative relationship'. She was faced with the choice of compromising her own citizenship at a time of war, or possibly losing her life and business partner for an indeterminate period, and chose the former. Ultimately the decision did not appear to have a big impact on their lives and, whether for political or professional reasons, by 1943 they were entrusted to handle MOI commissions directly.

John estimated that they made some 70 films during the war, many of them short, 90-second public information inserts in cinema newsreels about salvaging, allotment management, fuel economy and similar subjects. They also produced a series of anti-Nazi propaganda films in Arabic for the Middle East featuring a little boy called Abu; *Six Little Jungle Boys* (1945), warning soldiers of the dangers of foot rot, venereal disease and other dangers of the ongoing war in Asia; and a seven-part series on ship handling filmed in Technicolor which, if screened together, came the closest that Britain would come to an animated feature film for some years.

All of these films were made by a varying staff of fifteen to twenty people, mainly women, who worked together in a close-knit, almost family community through the wartime experience. One of those women, Vera Linnecar, found Joy very approachable in this period, and remembered her grinning in meetings behind John's back at his somewhat unique take on English pronunciation, refusing to correct his mistakes as she found them so adorable. The work seems to have been a true partnership at this stage, with the pair working collaboratively on the story, planning, scene breakdown, script and direction, and sharing credits. Joy later described their working methods as 'pretty similar, except we have this divergence on script. Because John was more keen on how the thing looks, and the production values and I kept on saying, "What does it matter if nobody knows what you are trying to say?"'

For a short period the studio moved out of London to Bushey, near Joy's birth town of Watford, perhaps because of the risk of bombing to their now essential wartime work. And yet they moved back to central London before the end of the war and set up their studio in the heart of Britain's film industry at 10A Soho Square, where

On March 13, 1938, Hitler marched into Vienna and annexed Austria. The proximity of the German army, the looming anti-Semitic climate and shutting down of funds from their backers meant that Joy and John left Budapest in June 1938 in a hurry. They had to borrow money to take one of the last trains back towards London and travelled 3rd class on wooden benches. On June 24, Joy wrote in her very sparsely filled diary just the words, 'German passport office' followed on June 26 by 'pay stops'.

they would remain for many years. After years of scrabbling for work there was now a constant, demanding stream of it, and the hours were long and hard, not without health effects on both John and Joy. A bomb which hit their Chelsea flat in 1941 left Joy buried up to the neck in rubble, resulting in enduring back pain and depression. Joy said 'The full effects of the bombing came out over twenty years later. At the time I thought little of the vertigo and blackouts that followed soon after. In 1943 I had a miscarriage under the impression that I had appendicitis I had mild depression after'.

But their wartime efforts were rewarded in the post-war period by further government commissions, including a seven-part series of films featuring a character called Charley which were designed to communicate many of the ground-breaking socialist policies of the new Labour regime. *Charley's March of Time* (1948), for example, presented the difficult task of not just communicating facts about the government's new national insurance scheme, but also create a cogent and convincing case for accepting short term pain for long-term gain.

The biggest difference from the wartime work, however, was that Joy now had to work more from home amidst the demands of a baby daughter, Vivien, born in 1945. 'The Halas & Batchelor was no longer fifty-fifty', she later wrote. 'I was, as a witty friend remarked, literally left holding the baby. John was holding the studio together and

Soon after the outbreak of war they secured contracts with the Admiralty, the War Office and the Ministry of Information for the production of instructional and propaganda films and have been continuously engaged on this work since. They still have contracts with the Admiralty, the War Office and the Central Office of Information, which applicant states, will occupy their output for at least another year. The existence of these contracts has been confirmed.

On the 3rd March, 1944 applicant formed a private limited liability company called HALAS & BATCHELOR CARTOON FILMS, LTD., with a nominal capital of £1,000 in £1 shares (certificate of incorporation No.386578). Only two shares have been issued and are held by applicant and his wife. HALAS states that he will continue his present activities as a firm so long as he is engaged on Government contracts and the above mentioned company will not function until he enters the ordinary film market.

On the 27th April, 1940 in London, HALAS was married to Joy Ethel BATCHELOR a British born woman, who has already been referred to in this report as his business partner. This woman re-acquired British nationality by the grant of a certificate of naturalization on the 28th December, 1945 (certificate No. D.Z.3151 H.O. Ref. H. 6829/3).

Both applicant and his wife were exempted from the special restrictions imposed on enemy aliens by Article 6a and 9a of the Aliens Order, 1920 as amended (H.O. letter 6829/2 dated the 27th July, 1943).

The alien has an adequate knowledge of the English language.

There is no evidence to show that he has ever been connected with any foreign subversive organisation and he does not appear to interest himself in extreme politics. He expresses loyal sentiments towards this country.

The conviction mentioned in Para 14(i) of the application form is confirmed by police records and nothing further is disclosed to his detriment. Nothing is shown to the detriment of his wife.

Inspector

SUPERINTENDENT

On their return to London John was faced with possible internment. To make sure he could stay in London and work on films for the government Joy married John in 1940. To her dismay she found that she was now considered Hungarian and a 'friendly enemy alien', and so, like John, was subject to a curfew. She did not regain her British citizenship until 1945. (see previous page)

While Joy was giving birth, John was also in hospital having his appendix out. Concerned for him, Joy wrote John daily letters containing drawings of the room, the nurses and Vivien. She also wrote instructions for the studio. Their exchange of letters was neatly kept in a bundle and tied with a blue ribbon, found later in her bedroom cupboard.

my life was never the same again, nor probably was his.' Becoming a mother may have changed the working pattern in the relationship, yet Joy continued to focus on the company - there are letters giving instructions to the company written on the day Vivien was born.

As a baby, Vivien was sent to a weekly boarding nursery, returning home at weekends, and was frequently cared for by her grandparents. Joy concentrated more on the pre-production stages like scripts and storyboards which could be done at home, but these were always her strengths in the partnership. Whilst she continued to work at the studio itself to direct animators and the other creatives, her presence is always more fleeting and elusive than John's in people's memories.

The distinction that Joy later put on the divide was that John became the main contact point and producer of the company because it involved travelling, visits and socialising. He became the primary figure associated with the company, and increasingly the British animation industry as a whole. He was the face that people saw, and he was a good storyteller, politician and showman.

It is interesting that this was also the period when the studio's first 'art' film was released, the ten-minute abstract visual ballet *Magic Canvas* (1948). Joy is uncredited on the film – the kind of production that would gain more critical acclaim than the sponsored works. A son, Paul, was added to the mix in 1949, and the family moved to Hampstead so that they could be closer to the Soho studio.

The needs of the company were growing along with the family as John and Joy embarked on their best-known film, the feature-length animated version of George Orwell's *Animal Farm* (1954). The film was something of a commission from the American producer Louis De Rochement, whose attention they had gained with their sponsored works such as *The Shoemaker and the Hatter* (1949), made to promote the Marshall plan. The surreptitious financing of the film, involving contributions and some editorial input by what was effectively the CIA, has been discussed in depth elsewhere. Regardless of its background, John and Joy jumped wholeheartedly into the adventure and it was a project for which they shared a great passion.

Joy's contribution to the scripting, development and characterisation of the film was immense, particularly in the early stages when the work mostly took place at home. Joy tried to work around the needs of the children, insisting on an early breakfast together as a family, and spending two hours each evening with the children for tea, stories and bed, making up the hours at evenings and weekends. And yet Joy travelled back and forth to New York in this period, sometimes for up to a month at a time whilst her mother stayed with the children and was clearly still fulfilling the 'production' role that she felt she lacked. It is where the work stepped into the rapidly expanding studio – or very soon studios – and was delegated to a burgeoning number of staff that Joy may not have been able to make the contribution she wanted, and felt left aside. Pictures of the film in production often feature John at the heart of discussions, whereas Joy's presence survives more in the many script drafts, covered in her handwritten annotations, and in the correspondence with the film's backers. When interviewed in later life Joy stated that it was the film that she enjoyed working on most.

After *Animal Farm* the company was perfectly positioned to take advantage of the arrival of commercial television in Britain, making over 200 television commercials in the first full year of ITV, 1956. At the same time they were picking up commission after commission from large companies who were investing in lavish sponsored films rather than hand their profits to the government, due to a post-war tax loop of the time. Despite this success, it was here that a divide truly seemed to set in. The fact that the partnership was no longer fifty-fifty, as Joy put it, did not mean that she was doing less, but that in fact she was taking on a heavier burden in the relationship. She still put in her fifty per cent of efforts towards the company, but on top of that she took on the role of mother with more commitment than John seemed to give to being a father. On the back of the damage and demands of her wartime experience over ten years of such a double life put a strain on Joy that would come back to haunt her health in the coming years, mentally as well as physically.

Outside of *Animal Farm*, the reputation of the Halas & Batchelor today is largely based on the independent 'free films' that were made for themselves rather than commissioned by sponsors. John does appear to be the primary driver behind these works, as with the *Magic Canvas* mentioned earlier, and Joy's role in these films is harder to pick apart. She stated that she initially 'manned' the *History of the Cinema* (1957), a ten-minute satire on the growth of film and television, but the final film credits John alone as director and producer, and he shares script and design credits with Nick Spargo and Ted Pettingell respectively. Joy is uncredited. She has a script credit on *Automania 2000* (1963), the first British animation to gain an Oscar nomination, and she later wrote about the more improvisational, collaborative approach they took to the creative process behind the film. But again she has no credit for design, production or direction.

The start of the 1960s saw a diversion from the norm as Halas & Batchelor produced their second feature film, one of the very few live-action films they made, the *Monster of Highgate Ponds* (1961). Funded by the Children's Film Foundation, the film was based on a story by Joy (who also designed the monster), and directed by Alberto Cavalcanti, whose unusual career encompassed periods as part of the Parisian avant-garde of the 1920s, the British documentary film movement of the 1930s, and Ealing Studios in the 1940s. Whilst the production must have been a novel distraction, in retrospect Joy was fairly dismissive of the project, and even the stop-motion sequences of the juvenile monster in the film did not offer the same rewards as drawn animation for her. She later wrote of John and the company that, 'By the end of the 1950s our interests and films began to diverge. The process continued through the 1960s: a succession of boring film subjects that fell to my lot had left me bored and didn't improve the films. The realisation that I lacked experience and skill in all the political, business and social "games" that go with film-making, resulted in long tedious illnesses and a great creative loss.'

True or not, Joy certainly felt that she had been left to deal with the bread-and-butter sponsored film commissions that had first established the company's reputation, and were the true source of income, and yet were generally artistically unsatisfying after over twenty years in business. The fact that John was going from strength to strength in his reputation domestically, and then internationally through his role at ASIFA, the International Animated Film Association founded in 1960, added to the sense of neglect, even though she too was one of the founder members.

John's first published writing on animation in English was a joint essay with Joy for the *Penguin Film Review* in the 1940s, but his many subsequent books on animation were all undertaken with a series of different collaborators and never again with his wife and business partner. And yet Vivien Halas recalls him asking her mother's opinion on everything he did, clearly respecting her advice and knowledge, and that he 'lost the plot entirely' when she died.

Strains on their relationship led to distractions outside of it for both parties, increasing the tensions. The medications that went along with the succession of illnesses that plagued Joy through this period did not mix well with an over-reliance on drink as a stress reliever and social lubricant. Whilst John was directing *Hamilton the Musical Elephant* (1961) and *Automania 2000* (1963), and dealing with a series of children's television series like *Foo-Foo* (1960), Joy was left directing films on the Commonwealth and its Columbo Plan, and producing a film called *Sputum* (1965). She found increasingly that she could get more pleasure from taking time off animation to work in the garden, and yet she was launched into three years of work on an adaptation of Gilbert and Sullivan's *Ruddigore,* released in 1964.

Made for American television, at 54 minutes *Ruddigore* was the company's longest animated feature since *Animal Farm*, and yet it was made with a tenth of the personnel and so can suffer in comparison. Joy later wrote that she embarked on the project reluctantly and thought she would be sharing the direction, but John became involved in the *Tales of Hoffnung* series (1964) for the BBC instead. Knowing the limitations, and accepting that abridging one of Gilbert and Sullivan's more minor works is a difficult starting point, the final film is often charming. This is clearly Joy's film, with character designs exhibiting traits back to her work in the 1940s. Even if she entered the project half-heartedly, the poor critical reception must have been personally hard to take.

In the early 1960s Halas & Batchelor established an off-shoot company, the Educational Film Centre (EFC), which as the name suggests specialised in films for classrooms and other learning environments. Ten years on from 1955, the golden age for British animation production kickstarted by the arrival of commercial television was beginning to wane, as were the large-scale sponsored commissions due to changes in business taxation. The impetus of Halas & Batchelor as a company was beginning to wane, alongside Joy's enthusiasm for the business. The new business opportunity was felt to be American television cartoons, either self-initiated such as *Dodo The Kid from Outer Space* (1964-65) for which they produced over 70 episodes in quick time, or outsourced commissions such as the King Features Syndicates, *Popeye the Sailor* series (1960-62). John and Joy decided that to keep the business running required new investment and they sold the majority of the company to Tyne Tees Television, keeping a 20 per cent stake. Their influence in the company that still carried their name fell rapidly, and what Joy referred to as the 'new empire' at the company rejected and even maligned the style of past work in order to promote a new house brand.

Under the Halas & Batchelor banner Joy directed a film about foot health called *The Five* (1970), with an ingenious approach of bringing characterisation to toes and successfully mixed the past and then-present styles of the company.

Less successful were pilot children's programmes *Bolly in a Space Adventure* (1968) and *The Wotdot* (1970). The situation with the ownership company came to a head in 1972, when John and Joy felt that they were forced to release their remaining shares in the company under false pretences. Much of the stressful fallout from this situation fell to Joy to deal with, as John was away at an International Council of Graphic Design Associations (Icograda) congress - another international commitment that John had joined up to in 1964, much to Joy's distress. Interestingly, in her letters to their legal council Joy signs herself as Mrs Joy Halas. In the same year her daughter moved away to live in Paris, and Joy began to feel significant arthritis in her hands.

Joy continued working for a period using other artists like the Hungarian Janos Kass to draw and complete the storyboards that she could no longer produce to her satisfaction. One of the films produced by this method was *Contact* (1973), a seventeen-minute history of the development of electricity, produced under the EFC banner for a French company. The film is a tour de force of state-of-the-art animation film-making, using computer assistance and a remarkably slick, modern design. It received a number of international awards and managed to find some audience beyond its limited original intended market. By 1974 Joy had effectively retired from film-making.

In 1975, John and Joy were able to buy Halas & Batchelor back, but Joy stepped away from production. She kept her hand in animation by teaching at the London International Film School, something she very much enjoyed (she also acted as a governor for many years), and continued to be a presence on the international animation scene. The company would be sold and bought again, adding to the stresses of what should have been more restful years.

Different people have different memories of Joy from this period, until her death in 1991. The long, exhausting career had left her body ready for retirement, even if her mind was not, but her husband showed no signs of stopping. Tiredness often leads to bitterness, and her sharp wit could often become caustic, leading to a feisty reputation and distancing some who may have become closer. And yet others could experience her warmth and generosity of spirit, like French animator Monique Renault, who met Joy at the Cambridge Animation Festival in 1985. She described 'Madame Batchelor' as one of the women who changed her life; kind, respectful and a real lady, giving her the encouragement to go on in her career despite the odds.

Joy was certainly the woman who changed the British animation industry the most, and for the better. Her professionalism, perspective and tireless

This is Joy, ever elegant, in a Christian Dior hat with ASIFA and festival friends in Annecy. In the early 1960s there was always a picnic that gave everyone a chance for informal exchanges. Joy was very convivial and both she and John enjoyed giving cocktail and dinner parties.

effort was a key driving force in reinvigorating the moribund pre-World War Two British animation scene, to become an exciting and dynamic golden age for the industry in the 1950s.

Her career was umbilically linked to John's, and may not have reached such heights without him, but the opposite is almost certainly also true, and whatever the travails of their lives and careers, they should always be considered as a partnership. That she never completed her own 'great work' is a great shame, but perhaps not a surprise given the difficulties of the industry, and her support of the more forceful presence of her husband's vision. She talked about 'hugging the jewel' of an idea of making a series of films based on the Breton *Lais de Marie de France*, but they never came to fruition. Typically she put the work of the company above anything else, including her own ambitions, and as her result her life and work has become overshadowed. With this publication it is hoped that the light returns to the work of this remarkable lady.

A note on sources:
Joy wrote some of her biography in brief, unfinished documents at various stages of her life, and not always the happiest ones. She was also interviewed in 1988 by the industry union as part of what is now known as the BECTU History Project.
Other information comes from discussions with Vivien Halas, the book *Halas & Batchelor Cartoons: An Animated History*, and through working on the Halas & Batchelor Collection at the BFI National Archive.

A Woman's Place *Clare Kitson*

Joy Batchelor's animation career began in 1934. Sadly, during the period when I used to see her from time to time in around 1970, I missed my chance to interview her on the subject. Animation history was not my great interest at that time and even if it had been I would not have had the courage to interview Joy. She had a very sharp wit – deadly, in fact. I kept out of the firing line. I have only recently understood that she might, by that stage, have felt sidelined in the industry, embittered maybe – even though it was continually whispered that Joy, not John, was the creative talent in that couple.

By the time I did take an interest in women in animation, it was too late. Joy's entry into the animation industry came at a very propitious moment. It was a time when Britain was only just beginning to gear up to the kind of production-line system already in use in the US, where the processes and the hierarchical rankings were, from the bottom up: paint mixing, painting, tracing, checking, inbetweening, animating, directing. And animation was the only route to the director's role.

Joy is working on *Animal Farm* with Paul under her desk in this posed shot for *Woman's Weekly*.

One of Joy's illustrations for the *Animal Farm* book (right)

Needless to say, by the time the system really got going, the lower orders were occupied by women and it was a rare woman who got beyond checking. In 1934, however, it seems that only one British studio, Anson Dyer, had fully adopted this system. And Joy never worked there.

Joy had acquitted herself well at her local art school but had to refuse a scholarship to the Slade, since her family needed her to start earning. Realising she now had to abandon her ambitions in the fine art line, she started applying for jobs in animation - without any great enthusiasm, it must be said. And an Australian named Dennis Connelly gave her a job as inbetweener on the first of the two short films based on koala characters that he made in London. Joy had no training. She just 'found out', she said, how to do it. And she was immediately promoted to animator.

A decade later it would be unheard of for a woman to jump the lower ranks and start as an inbetweener. But in 1934 there were still so very few candidates with animation experience that lucky breaks like this were possible. An Australian newspaper, *The Argus*, reported with pride in September 1934 that 'fourteen specialists' - one of whom was presumably Joy - had worked on the koala film. A second reason, incidentally, that she was able to skip the lower ranks is that, judging from an interview she gave in 1989[1], most of those ranks did not exist at all in smaller outfits such as Dennis Connelly's. Animation, it seems, was not done on paper there, and then traced, but instead was done straight on to cell, in ink. It was messy work but, to her surprise, Joy now found animation extremely exciting.

In around 1937 she answered a small ad in the *Evening Standard,* and was accepted by John Halas to join his team of four making *Music Man*. It was a hand-to-mouth existence at that stage. Much of the production was done in the bohemian milieu of Budapest, but lack of finance and Hungary's increasing closeness to Nazi Germany meant they - and especially John, who was Jewish - had to retreat to London. In the absence of funding for animation, both had to rely on freelance design work for newspapers and magazines. As John still spoke very little English it was the talented, as well as beautiful, Joy who represented the couple, taking their work round to prospective clients and making valuable contacts. At that stage she was bursting with confidence.

When the war came, it brought both good and bad consequences for Joy. The pair's advertising work for J Walter Thompson was now supplemented by a regular stream of commissions from the Ministry of Information (MOI), all considered imperative for the war effort. This meant John was spared internment on the Isle of Man - which was to be the fate of most of the other so-called 'enemy aliens', many of whom were, like John, Jewish refugees from Nazism. He was nevertheless classed as an 'enemy alien', even though in a reserved occupation, which meant that since he and Joy were now married, the latter now became a 'friendly enemy alien', with the result that both of them had a strict curfew imposed. She was not to have her British nationality reinstated until the early 1950s. Another major problem for Joy was a back injury she sustained during the London bombing, causing her considerable pain while she persevered with work on those vital war effort productions.

But in career terms the war was an excellent time, as it was for many women in animation. Whereas after the war most would find themselves in paint-and-trace, during the war any woman who wanted to, and had the talent, could rise to the higher ranks, in the absence of the men who were away fighting. According to Denis Gifford's extremely useful bibliography of British animated films[2], Halas & Batchelor appears to have been the most woman-friendly of the studios, with John Halas and, occasionally, Harold Mack the only men featuring in the regular animation team that usually included Joy Batchelor, Vera Linnecar, Kathleen (Spud) Houston and Rosalie (Wally) Crook. Joy was also taking joint credit with John as producer, director and scriptwriter. The high point in this respect was the 1945 feature film for the Admiralty, *Handling Ships,* on which eleven of the sixteen animators were female.

Immediately after the war, the good times for women animators continued for a while. Halas & Batchelor continued with their mostly-female team on government-commissioned films, such as the *Charley* series, for the MOI (now renamed the COI), and the advertising work for J Walter Thompson now returned. One wonders though what Joy (as scriptwriter, co-director and

Joy with a set of *Animal Farm* porcelain figurines.

co-producer) and the all-woman animation team of Wally Crook, Spud Houston and Vera Linnecar thought of the subject-matter the client had clearly demanded for the Brooke Bond commercial *Dolly Put the Kettle On* (1949) - the tale of two female dolls competing for the love of a male teddy bear by careering around making endless cups of tea. Many of the other commercials featured equally demeaning roles for women. At this, early post-war stage some men had returned to the H&B animation team and animator Vera Linnecar remembers this as a particularly happy time. Yet things started to go wrong when somehow all the men were taken off into a separate unit, which tended to be given all the macho films, such as those for Anglo-Iranian

Outside 10A Soho Square
Part of the Halas & Batchelor team remembered by Vera as (left to right) Jacquie, Vera Linnecar, Elizabeth Horne, Beryl Stevens and Wally Crook.

The view from the studio
Soho Square in the snow around 1944, taken by Stella Harvey, one of the animators.

Early days at home
John, Joy and unidentified members of the team.

John with his harem
Vera Linnecar remembers this as a picnic to celebrate the wedding of studio members Doris Bevan (back row centre) and 'Pop' Bevan (on her left). On her right is Joy and in the front centre is John with Christine Jollant on his left, Liz Horne on his right and next to her Wally Crook. The others go unremembered.

Behind the scene
Stella Harvey remembers that the cameraman was 'a bit of a groper and we all dodged going in the dark room with him.'

oil, while the women continued alone, with films on 'women's' subjects. This is when Vera jumped ship for Larkins. It was also the time when Joy's career took a change in direction.

Before focusing specifically on Joy at this period, it is perhaps worth diverging for a moment to look at the situation for most women, and indeed take a look at how this compares with today. In a Skillset report of 2010 into women in the creative industries in the UK, one of the conclusions was that 'Women working in the creative media industries are under-represented, underpaid, and more highly qualified than their male counterparts.' The figures for animation appeared to be even more skewed than in the other creative industries. I do not have the benefit of such statistics for the period of Joy's activity at Halas & Batchelor, but I have spoken to some of the women who were active in the period and it is clear that the women were indeed underpaid – in that they were virtually all confined to the lower-grade jobs in paint-and-trace. (The department was affectionately known by the all-male animators at Gaumont-British as 'the haggery', elsewhere as 'the cattle corps'!) And I have a strong suspicion that they were more highly qualified. All the women I spoke to had studied at art school, but not all the men had. It was certainly possible for an enthusiastic young man to bypass that step and talk himself into a job inbetweening.

It is hard to put a finger on firm reasons. There may or may not have been bias on the part of male employers. Before interviewing a range of women who had been in animation in the late 1940s, 1950s and 1960s, I had assumed that such male bias had indeed been the reason that so very few women progressed. Vera Linnecar certainly encountered it in her struggle up from paint-and-trace through animation to direction. But rather more of the women said that the reverse was true. When the advent of commercial television in 1954 meant a stepping-up of commercials production, the Larkins studio, for example, made all their staff spend time learning the rudiments of all the various specialisations and specifically urged the paint-and-trace girls to consider trying to move into animation. But they would not. They were especially proud of their brush-tracing technique - which, it is true, was acknowledged to be hard to master - and felt the whole art of the film was in those immobile cells, not in the movement they generated. There was also a disinclination to leave the camaraderie of the paint-and-trace department for the higher echelons where, they told me, they saw a great deal more back-biting.

Then there is the knotty problem of women's unwillingness to go into areas needing technical aptitude. It is undeniable that the aeons when women were limited to purely domestic duties had a strong limiting effect on female expectations and aspirations. One of the senior contingent that I spoke to, who did manage to make it into the animation department, told me she always knew she had a peculiar brain for a woman! I doubt the female brain is physically any less developed than the male brain in the areas governing the mechanics of movement, but it might as well be, for women's aspirations in the technical area appear to be advancing at a snail's pace. One prominent male member of the current British animation industry, who shall remain anonymous, but who has a great deal of experience helping both young men and young women with their animation, reports noting female eyes regularly glaze over as the explanation progresses. Nowadays the ever-increasing automation in the various processes in animation production has raised new barriers. However, I am assured that a few more women apply for computer animation courses every year. This has to be a good sign.

But what *is* certain about animation in the UK is that it has mostly existed in smallish units, producing work that is labour-intensive and therefore correspondingly more expensive than live action. Needing, consequently, to fight for work, and for their existence, and to hold their budgets down, companies of this kind have maintained very few full-time staff, only hiring when the need arose and demanding long hours for that limited period. For women, once they have a family, this is no way to earn a living. This is the point at which they head off for more secure and more flexible sources of income.

Halas & Batchelor, though, due in part to its particular niche making government films during and just after the war, was relatively prosperous. And the British animation industry as a whole was in fact not in too bad a state (certainly in comparison with today) - and it was about to become rather more successful for a while, when commercial television was introduced in 1954. So no very great financial pressures distorted Joy's career path. Yet even so the birth of Vivien in 1945 and Paul three years later would gradually force Joy away from the centre of activity in the Halas & Batchelor studio and towards far more scriptwriting, which could be done at home. In notes dictated in the early 1970s for an article, which does not appear to have been published, she says that:

'Peace in Europe and our daughter had arrived within a few days of each other - as did the Atom Bomb: a major upheaval all round. The Halas and Batchelor relationship was no longer fifty-fifty. (…) John was holding the studio together and my life was never the same again. Nor, probably, was his. (…) Let no one suppose it was easy. (…) By the time our son was born I had learnt to organise a household and to start visits to the studio to work on scripts and storyboards at 6am; to pick items up where I had left off, at any time; to go without sleep, without much social life and be eternally grateful to my mother. Grandparents are great…'[3]

Joy certainly played an active and very enthusiastic role in the massive undertaking of the first British-made animated feature, *Animal Farm* (1954), but apart from that there now seemed to be less enthusiasm for those very few of the projects for which funding was forthcoming, which were allocated to Joy either to co-direct or to direct. Her major project, the feature film

Ruddigore (1964), on which she spent three years, was a thankless task due largely, she felt, to the inadequacies of the script that W S Gilbert had apparently knocked out in three weeks. One very intriguing, but sadly unfulfilled aspiration, which she mentions in an interview of 1989[4], was a series based on the twelfth-century lays (poems, probably intended to be sung) of Marie de France. These were revolutionary in their attitudes to love and the role of women, but the only interest shown by potential funders was in what they took to be the saucy title.

In 1960 the Annecy animation festival was born and suddenly there was a great deal of prestige to be had for short animated 'auteur' films that garnered prizes. This coincided with tremendous international success for British animated commercials and, consequently, a bit of spare cash in the British studios that they could spend on 'auteur' films. This was also the time when scriptwriter Stan Hayward came into his own. It was Stan who wrote *The Wardrobe* (1960), *The Flying Man* (1962) and *The Apple* (1962) for George Dunning; *Love Me, Love Me, Love Me* (1962) for Richard Williams; *Alf, Bill and Fred* (1964) and *Rope Trick* (1967) for Bob Godfrey; *The Question* (1967) for John Halas; and *Fairy Story* (1968) for Ron Wyatt and Tony Cattaneo, to name but a few. Yet while Stan wrote these celebrated works they were still personal to their directors in a very real sense, for Stan had an extraordinary knack of understanding each director and somehow producing the idea that fitted perfectly with the predilections and concerns of each of them. These films, laden with festival prizes, were tremendously influential in promoting the reputations of these filmmakers and of British animation in general. Years later Joy was to say of the British animation community that '… (those) who have something specific to say are few and far between. There is only one outstanding scriptwriter and that is Stan Hayward…'

Yet, somehow, in the 1960s, that crucial decade both for Joy Batchelor and for British animation, that link was never made. Stan did not happen, spontaneously, to have a Joy-Batchelor-style idea, and Joy never approached him to ask for one. It was only a good decade later that the two happened to have a conversation about Joy's career and her future direction. She asked Stan's advice as to whether she should pursue a scriptwriting consultancy that John had recommended her for. She was nervous. By that time, it seemed to Stan, all the confidence of that extraordinary woman who had once been the face, voice and major talent of Halas & Batchelor, had drained away.

References
[1] Interview by Kay Mander, 10 March 1989
[2] *British Animated Films, 1895-1985: A Filmography*. Pub. Denis Gifford, 1987, McFarland & Company, North Carolina, USA.
[3] Kay Mander interview op. cit
[4] Kay Mander interview op. cit

A personal view *Vivien Halas*

Joy started out believing that men and women were equal. Her mother had channelled her own frustrated ambitions into Joy with the idea that a woman's place was not necessarily in the home. She was told that hard work and talent would save her from the workhouse. So work hard she did, and with good results. Not many women were able to use their talents so effectively, developing a career as an animator, writer, director and producer, at a time when most women in animation worked as painters and tracers.

When I was little I thought of my mother as a completely wonderful, beautiful princess. I remember her swirling about in an elegant burgundy silk dress that I hung on to and had to be pulled off so that she could go out for the evening. I might not have been so clingy had I not been sent to a weekly boarding nursery when I was still a baby.

My earliest memory is of watching dancing telegraph wires, while lying on the backseat of the car and then clinging to my mother's yellow jacket and seahorse brooch, not wanting to be separated.

I recently found a cache of letters between Joy and John, neatly tied with a blue ribbon in one of the archive boxes. Joy was in a nursing home having just given birth to me, worried about John who was in hospital nearby having just had his appendix out. The year before, in 1944, he had collapsed from overwork and malnutrition due to the wartime diet. The letters show how involved she was with the day-to-day organisation and running of the studio and how she thought more about John than herself.

It never seemed to have occurred to her that having a child might interrupt their work. Joy had always seen herself as a bohemian, an artist with ambition, and said later, 'I was not looking for a husband but to find my place in the world.' In John she felt that she had met a soul mate, not just romantically but as an equal work partner with whom she could make a difference to the world. By sending me to the weekly nursery she was able to carry on as usual for a while, but later in an interview she told the documentary film-maker Kay Mander, 'I had to leave animation, work in studio and directing and production, I took up scriptwriting because you can't have children and hop into the studio each day, and that's when I really began to write scripts.' The separation from the day-to-day studio life left her feeling isolated and, for the first time, the Halas and Batchelor partnership felt less than equal.

Vera Linnecar, one of the animators who worked at Halas's, as they called it during the war, told me in an interview, 'Joy was very shy, workaholic and a perfectionist but approachable and fun. We used to go to parties at their house and have ping pong tournaments, everyone in the studio was invited. Joy showed me some beautiful drawings that she'd made of herself pregnant.' Vera also recalled that '...we never knew when we left the studio if our homes would still be there when we got back because of the bombing.'

Another member of the team, Christine Jollant, who was recruited as a paint-and-tracer by Joy in the war, from her old Watford Art school, age fifteen, told me 'I loved it so much at Halas's that I stayed for ten years. Everyone was so friendly and Joy was beautiful, I remember how she worked right through both pregnancies, smoking away all the time. We worked at Bush House and every time there was an air raid we would get under our desks, even John and Joy did, and when it was over we would just carried on working.' This phone conversation was especially interesting to me, as Joy had always stressed that she never smoked or drank during her pregnancies!

John and Joy were bombed one night in their Chelsea flat. John was lucky but Joy said, 'I was buried up to the neck in rubble whilst John was more or less untouched as he happened to be standing in the doorway. The full effects of the bombing came out over twenty years later. At the time I thought little of the vertigo and blackouts that followed soon after.'

This was the seed of her troubles, as her medical history shows. She wrote it with John's help whilst in hospital trying to come to terms with illness, depression and alcohol misuse. As a child I was often frightened that she would die in the night, such as the time she had double pneumonia and the hospital delivered oxygen canisters to the house so that she could breathe.

After the birth of my brother Paul in 1949 we moved from Northwood Hills in Middlesex, where we had lived next door to my grandparents, to Hampstead, to be nearer to the studio in Soho. After three years living in a flat we moved again, to a modernist single storey house, both of them just opposite Hampstead Heath, and within walking distance of John and Joy's émigré colleagues such as Matyas Seiber, who composed the music for *Animal Farm*. In those days Hampstead was a village and not at all expensive. John and Joy could now afford a series of live-in au-pair girls to look after us, and Joy was able to organise her work between home and the studio. She would write out long, detailed lists of instructions to the home helps, listen to their problems (one young Swedish girl needed help in fending off perverts on the Heath) and still find time for tea and bedtime stories with us.

During the making of *Animal Farm* Joy would travel to New York with John, leaving Paul and me with our grandmother, who, although kind, brought a no-nonsense discipline into our lives. I was not good with authority and one of the worse moments of my life up until then was when I slipped out of the front gate to play with a friend for just a little too long and she called the police. Her anger frightened me so much that, to my shame, I never admitted where I had been and pretended that I had been hiding behind the garden shed. This made things even worse and I got a taste of how an adult could become hysterical when hurt and how things might have been for Joy.

Animal Farm was a pivotal time (1951-1955) for Halas & Batchelor. Both Joy and John felt that here at last was a worthwhile project after all the years of making short films for the government on a shoestring budget.

Joy was hailed as 'The Woman Disney' and there were journalists all over the studio and our house taking photos for magazines. Joy thought all this was fairly patronising, as the press seemed to take more interest in her as a homemaker than a film-maker, but on the whole she enjoyed the attention and so did John.

Dinner at the Dorchester to celebrate the completion of *Animal Farm*. From left to right John Halas, Joy Batchelor, Borden Mace and Sonia Orwell (Blair).

The Herbert family
Joy's mother Ethel, the little girl on the left, was brought up with strict Victorian values. Next to her is her father, an artificer who died young from an industrial accident, her favourite brother, who died young at sea and her older sister Flo who according to Ethel was 'lazy' but outlived them all. Far right is her mother who looks stern but was very kind and supportive to Joy as she grew up.

Ethel and Edward Joseph Batchelor
Joy's parents Ethel and Joe. It was a true love match but meant that Ethel had to give up her career managing the Northwood Golf Club.

Joy as a baby
Joy was born in 1914, a month before the outbreak of World War One. Joy suffered - her parents, recently married, made no secret of the fact that they really wanted a boy.

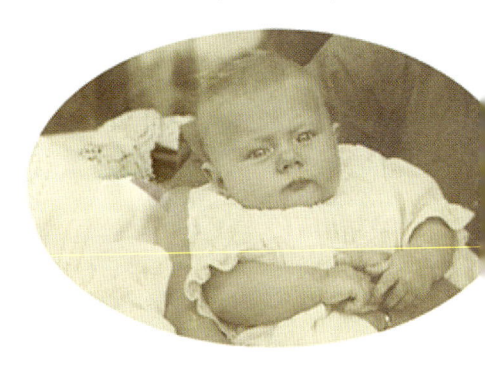

Joy in 1926
A posed shot of Joy with her favourite toy - later she said 'I prefer making dolls to playing with them'.

Joy with her grandmother
After the death of her brother Joy spent most of her holidays with her grandmother. Joy wrote 'the birth of my sister and the death of my brother caused quite an upheaval. My grandmother came to the rescue as she always did. My mother went away for a time and when she came home after a breakdown she was never the same again.'

Family walk
Family holidays were taken at Illfracombe in Devon. Here are Joy, Ethel, Joe and Barbara stepping out. Joy would show me this photo often and tell me about her many admirers.

Joy as a toddler
Ethel punished Joy for minor crimes by locking her in the cupboard under the stairs. Joy pretended that she loved this little cubbyhole and its comforting smells. She told herself stories developing her sense of fantasy and narrative. It also fuelled her wish to escape, shine and be different.

Joy with John
'My brother John was born when I was two. My mother had always wanted a boy and made no secret about it. I remember that he could be very funny and had a temper. No doubt he was spoilt and, no doubt about it, I was jealous. I even wished he would die.'

Joy and John at the seaside
John died of diphtheria aged four, just after the birth of Joy's sister Barbara in 1921. Joy wrote later 'I remember feeling guilty because I wasn't crying when everyone else was.'

Joy on the beach
Here is Joy posing for her long-term boy friend 'Pem'. I never did get to know his first name. She wrote 'By sixteen I had to my surprise become a very attractive girl with an outstanding figure and boys appeared from all directions.'

Lake Lucerne
John's brother Joseph, an architect, and his wife lived in Zurich. Joy was introduced to the family and they all spent time boating on Lake Lucerne.

Joy and Janos (John)
This photo must have been taken by Joseph or his wife Ruth, on the same holiday some time in 1938.

It must also be said that she became a good cook and a great party giver. Initially it was John who cooked but as time passed she took an interest in cooking and gardening. She read all manner of books on the subject and grew what were then considered unusual vegetables, such as purple sprouting broccoli and mange-tout peas, as well as carrying out romantic ideas such as sewing a thyme lawn... that came to a sad end when we cut it and a toad in two by mistake. She not only taught me to cook but to always be on the lookout for new recipes and the best ingredients. Much of her early work as an illustrator was for a series of cookery books by Josephine Terry, who devised post-war recipes to make do with scarcities: *Cook Happy*, *The Key to Cooking* and *Tell me Chef*. My first sex education came through another book that she illustrated in 1948, *The Truth about Stork*.

Joy took great pleasure in reading and researching ideas for new films. After the success of *Animal Farm* there were plans for other features with DeRochemont Films: *John Bunyan's A Pilgrims Progress*, *A Midsummer's Nights Dream* and her favourite, *Lais de Marie de France*. Sadly these projects never came to anything through lack of either interest or funding. Joy pointed out to me how many of these early precursors of the novel were written by women: Marie de France, Maria Edgeworth and Anne Radcliffe for example.

Living with Joy was to have a book club at home - not just women writers but other favourites such as Shakespeare, Walter de la Mare, Robert Graves, Graham Green and Laurence Durrell to list just a few. Life for men was easier, she told me at a tender age, and she wished that she had been born a man to better make her way in the world.

While Joy was alive I thought I knew her because our relationship felt so close, but since I have spent from 1996 taking care of the Halas & Batchelor archives, researching and preserving my parents'

work while bringing up my own daughter, I realise that closeness does not always give insight. For instance I never thought it odd that Joy would serve dry Martinis out of her bedroom cupboard!

You could have the best chats with Joy. I often felt I was on the verge on understanding 'the meaning of life' when talking with her, and even imagined that I knew about everything from the Greek myths to gardening until she finally died. In fact the thing I miss most about her is not being able to ask her about any subject, literature or nature or art or anything at all.

I once called her from France while staying in Picardy with friends and asked her what tree could be flowering in the winter woods with small yellow flowers? 'Cornus Mass dear, it's a kind of dogwood.' In the days before the Internet she was my source of all information. Even as she exploded and died of a ruptured stomach ulcer she was reading Robert Graves's *Anger of Achilles*. It was a traumatic moment. I was there; it was at 3am and I was five months pregnant. She called for help and as I picked her up with John's help, she was angry. 'Don't waste time cleaning up, get me to the toilet.' I rang for an ambulance and somewhere in all the panic came her last breath; a good girl to the end, she called out 'I'm finished'. As we waited numbly for the ambulance John found the illustrated copy of *Animal Farm* and showed me the difference between their drawings. 'All the good ones were hers', he said, 'you can see the difference in line, hers is more fluid and she was more talented than me.'

Here on a lighter note is a memory of Joy from a type designer friend, Geoff Halpin, with whom I worked in Hull when I was very young. He wrote:

'I met Joy in 1968 when she came up north to visit Vivien who I was working with at the time. It was my first design job after leaving college and I was not very worldly, having never been out of the North of England. Joy made a big impression; she was the most sophisticated person that Linda, my wife and I had ever met. Her caustic humour and wit were quite unlike anything we had experienced with anyone of our parents' generation.

Later we moved south and renewed our friendship with Vivien who had by then returned to work in London. Joy and John would often invite us to dinner with Vivien at their amazing modernist house on the edge of Hampstead Heath. Joy would usually be sitting by the fireplace with a glass of whisky in one hand and a Benson & Hedges in the other. While John was pouring small glasses of wine for everyone, Joy would tell us about her life in Hungary before the war and all the artists and designers she had known.

She told us about leaving Budapest quickly and coming back to England, as war seemed imminent. On the train journey, after seeing carriages loaded with German troops going the other way, they had to change trains and were forced to spend the night in Germany. To pass the time they went to a nightclub but immediately regretted it because almost everyone there was wearing Nazi uniform.

At one dinner party the conversation turned to fashion, more specially lingerie through the ages. We all agreed that the 1950s were the golden age. Joy left the room, then returned with a small collection of very stylish bras and suspender belts. As she showed them to us she recounted when and where she bought them and would occasionally say, I had a good time in that one. Then to our amazement she donated them to Linda, who was eventually also able to say, I had a good time in that one.'

When we were young Joy used to tell us exciting stories that she made up, but professionally she was ruthlessly critical, suspicious of pretention and just waiting to pounce on pomposity. However, like John, she was immensely kind to young hopefuls and always ready to encourage them. She would spend hours listening and chatting to the teenage son of a friend who was not getting on with his parents and lived with us for a while, and gave a college friend of mine such sound advice that she claimed it saved her marriage by saying: 'My dear I think you expect too much out of marriage. It is all about compromise.'

It must also be said that from around 1972 she had terrible arthritis that stopped her from drawing. So there she was, getting drawn into a life of illness, trying her best to get John to retire from the studio, the very thing that he loved, so that they could travel more or live in a Mediterranean climate, but finding that the best she could do was to create a garden in wet Wiltshire, not far from the Stroud studio. Instead of a house in Majorca their weekends were spent at their damp cottage, where she gardened and cooked and entertained while John wrote articles and books, sitting on the sofa, furthering the cause of animation.

Joy always joked that when she got old she wanted to be a bad-tempered old lady in a wheelchair who would whack people with her walking stick. As in the stories she used to tell us when we were very young, beware what you wish for. By the time she was 70 she had emphysema and her legs swelled up so badly that she did indeed spend much of her time in a wheelchair, or lying in bed reading. One day, two teenage boys tried to climb through her bedroom window from the garden.

Undaunted, Joy jumped out of bed and whacked them hard with her stick. They ran off in shock.

After her early ambitions Joy was in the end bound by the idea that she was an applied artist rather than an 'artist'. Her subversive nature possibly stopped her from fully enjoying her own work. Her films were all made for a purpose and her ideas of story-telling were rigorous; she believed in a beginning, middle and an end.

Joy may not have lived up to her early potential but was nevertheless one of the founder members of the Association Internationale du Film d'Animation (ASIFA), an honorary member of both the British Kinematograph Sound and Television Society, and the Society of Industrial Artists and Designers, and served on countless animation festival juries, as well as teaching and becoming a governor of the London International Film School. Right to her last moments her mind was razor sharp and she made a bold attempt to be equal in an unequal world.

A note on sources:
Most material comes from Joy's personal diaries and letters and my personal recollections. Other information comes from interviews with animators, Vera Linnecar, Stella Harvey, Christine Jollant, and friends Bridget Heal, Geoff and Linda Halpin and Richard Oliver.

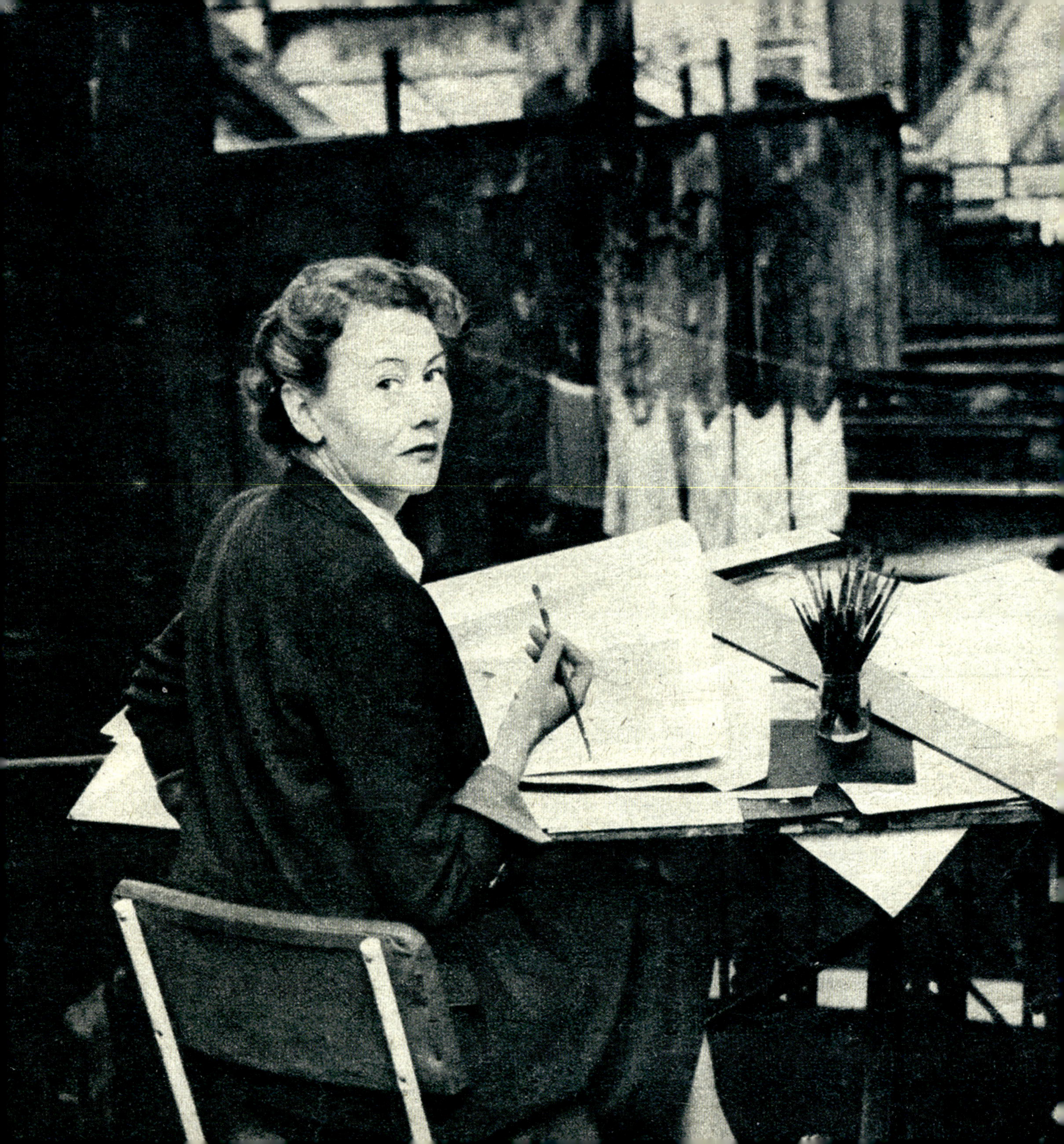

A gifted illustrator *Jim Walker*

Joy Batchelor was born in 1914 and spent her formative years in Watford, a creative community that had developed around the expanding printing industry. The prevailing smell and texture of printers' ink remained ever present for Joy, reinforced via her father, a master lithographer at John Bale & Danielson Ltd in Clerkenwell. Her father regularly brought home offcuts of prints and paper for Joy, who remembers him providing her with lots of drawing paper. It is clear that there was a close relationship with her father, one that could be described as a unity in creativity. As Joy notes:

'He was a great companion when I was small. Later on he provided endless supplies of drawing paper, taught me to plant and dig, to ride my bicycle, take it to pieces and put it back together again, to take photographs and develop and print them. Under his guidance I learnt to do lettering and to him I owe what talent I have for drawing.'

Joy working on *Animal Farm* in the Paddington studio, and an illustration for *Vogue* magazine. (right)

Joy's aquatint, designed and printed at Watford Art School, and fashion drawings for *Harpers* magazine (overleaf)

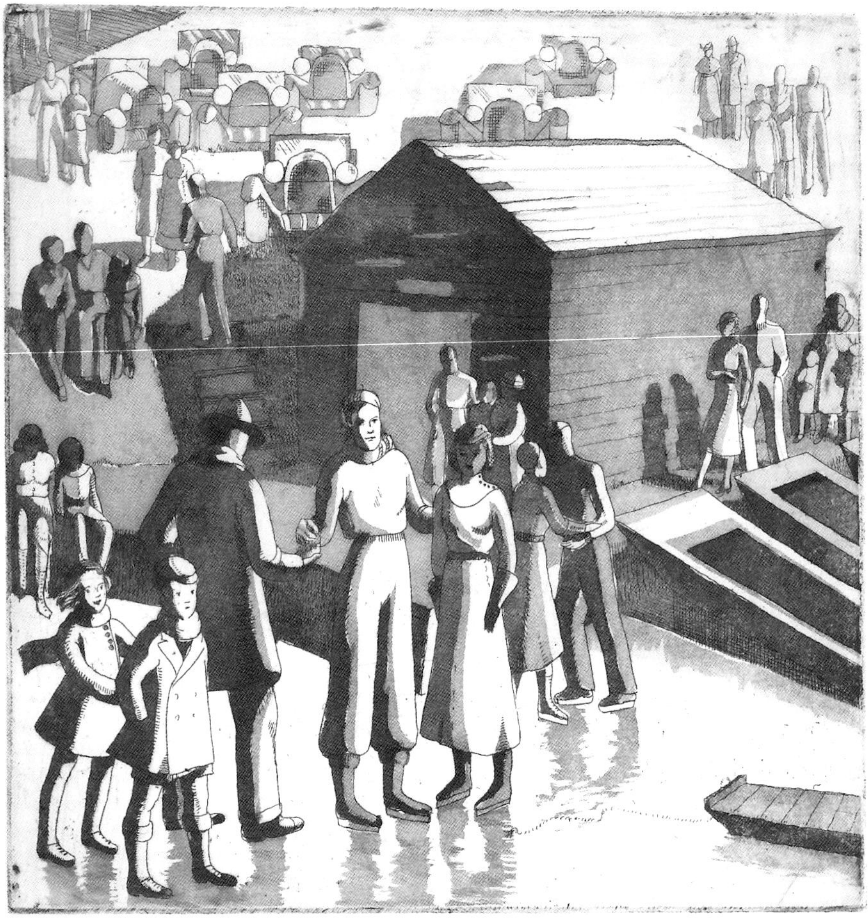

Drawing became a fundamental element and expressive medium for Joy, enabling her to creatively process ideas, but more importantly interrogate what she saw. There is an analytical aspect to her work that unravels what is perceived and reconstructed for the viewer, inviting them to engage and respond to the visual. It is this observational ability that makes Joy's early drawings and prints so evocative and full of dramatic potential. Two early prints show a structural narrative that reflects an engagement with her community and environment that echoes that of Stanley Spencer's early work. In a way they function as a commentary on an industrial and creative community. Both show strong observational skills and a creative desire to evoke narratives on everyday life. In particular, the view overlooking the back gardens is evocative of the domestic life that she knew.

The aquatint of people ice-skating is informed by a critical understanding of the compositional and structural staging of pre-Renaissance artists such as Giotto and later British artists, Stanley Spencer, Paul Nash, Eric Ravilious and Edward Bawden. The background is brought forward to create a dramatic sense of an unfolding landscape. The modelling and tonal forms of the figures present a lifelikeness that enhances the humanistic quality of their gestures. Joy shows a maturity and confidence in the expressive use of the line as a narrative form in her prints that is also present in her drawings and commercial work. In 1913 Joseph Pennell noted the potential impact of lithography on illustration and reproducing the expressive quality of the original drawing without the mediation of an engraver/printmaker.

These developments helped liberate the illustrator, as evidenced in the work of Edward Bawden, Eric Ravilious, Pearl Binder and Enid Marx. This led to a shift in the visual language of British illustration in the early twentieth century, informed by developments in printmaking and new forms of mechanical reproduction. This is visible in the fluid line seen in Joy's commercial and animation work, reflecting a conscious desire for a clear communicative image. There is an expressive energy in her sketches of Ross-on-Wye and the landscape illustrations for the illustrated edition of *Animal Farm*, both produced in the 1950s. This conscious awareness of the communicative potential of different qualities of line perhaps has

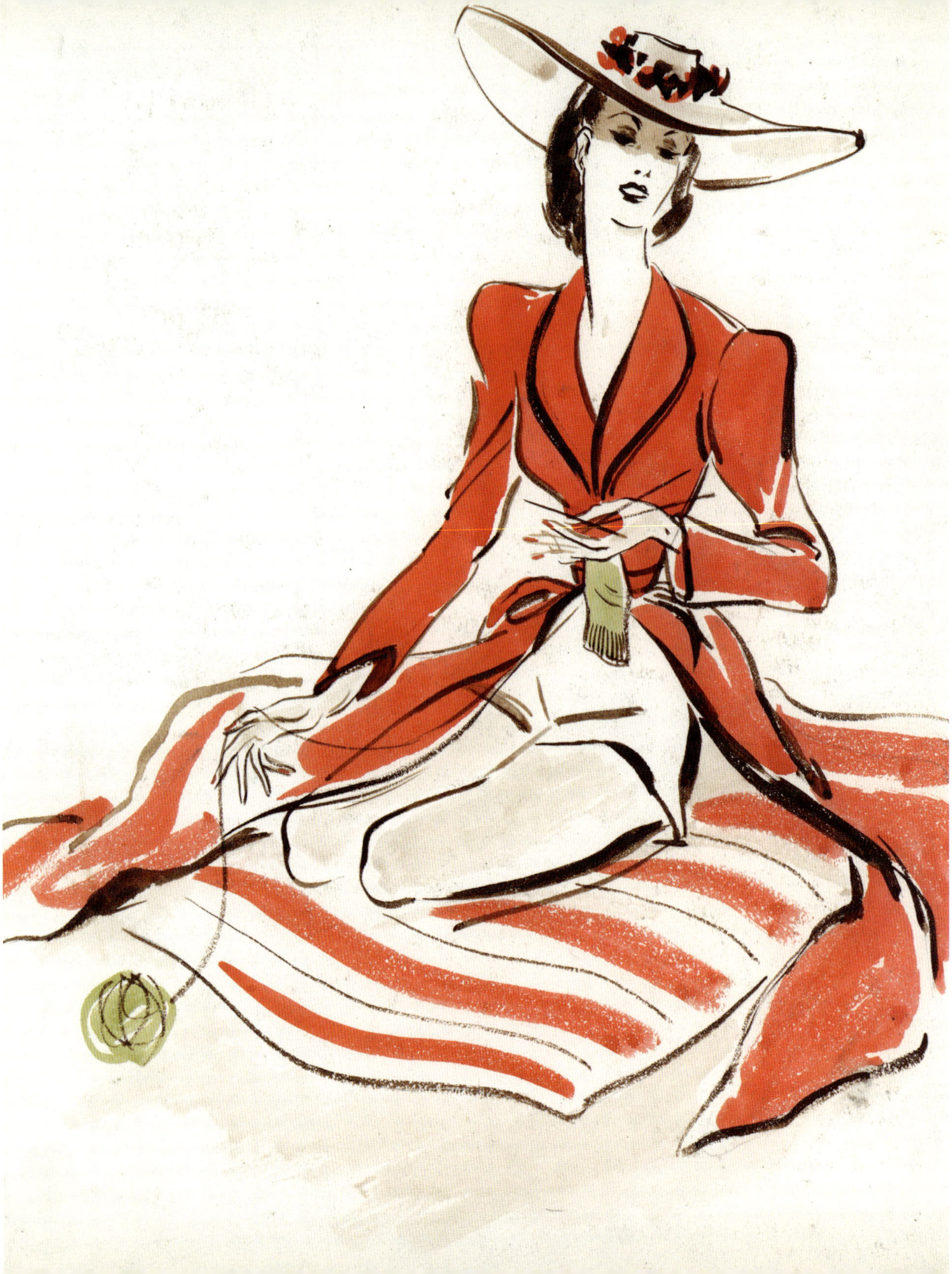

its foundation in printmaking and the skills taught to her by her father.

This difference in line perhaps presents a paradox in the functionality of the illustrative and animated line that lies in relation to its reproductive ability. As Sean Cubitt (2005) notes, animation required a consistent uniformity of line that functioned as both indicator of form and character to enable its repetition by key-animators and inbetweeners.

The fluidity of line in Joy's fashion illustrations and for Josephine Terry's recipe books focuses on characterisation that draws on the line as a compositional form echoing the brush marks of sumi-e painting. This fluidity is reflected in her film work, information films such as *Charley* (1947), *Dustbin Parade* (1941), *Jungle Warfare* (1943) and *Export or Die* (1946), where the contrasting width and form of the line add weight and dynamism to the characters. Even a frozen scene is full of dynamic potential, communicated via the lines of the character. This is also used effectively in animated commercials *Dolly Put the Kettle On* (1947) and *What's Cooking* (1949).

A study of Joy's preliminary sketches for her illustrations highlight the constant reflection on the effectiveness of the drawing through the overlapping pencil marks. With each gesture and mark we are able to follow her process of creative reductionism to bring to life the essence of a woman applying perfume. The highlighted inked elements signify the completion of the line and its unity with the image. Joy used brushwork

Fashion drawings for a womans' magazine (left) and a silk screen scarf designed by Joy on her return from Hungary, illustrating popular anti-German songs made famous by Flanagan & Allen, 1939.

for her commercial illustrations as functional compositional guides and cues for the viewer. This is evocatively presented in the domestic naturalness of the instructive filler for an article on 'How to bath in a bowl of water'. The domestic subject matter and settings of her commissions often presented Joy with an opportunity to evoke a joyful humour conveyed through the fluidity of the line in fillers for the *Daily Mail* and other publications. The illustration of a woman relaxing on a chair on a floor becomes alive through Joy's brushwork, in which the simplicity of line defines the form.

THE DAILY MIRROR — Tuesday, October 1, 1940

How to bath in a bowl of water

Photograph shows how you used to revel—up to your neck in soap. Sketch shows how you have to manage now... up to your ankles only. THEODORA BENSON tells you how to make the very best of this bowl business.

I WAS once privileged to meet a famous and rather romantic-looking Arctic explorer, with blazing blue eyes and everything according to schedule.

He told me that one of his exploration hardships was shortage of drinking water.

But, in spite of this and the more obvious hardship of cold, never, my hero assured me, did he neglect personal cleanliness.

"Every single day," he told me impressively, "I set aside a teacup of water to wash in!"

I know this ought to have given me a vision of the exterior of the fearless explorer's exertions, and of self-respect in the face of fearful odds.

But somehow I find it difficult to take it so. It's the idea of that hearty splendid chap, that man having a wash in a teacup that remained in my mind as comic.

Well, maybe it isn't quite so funny now I...

'I get along without you very well'
says CECILE LAVIGNE

ONCE the idea has penetrated, getting used to going without becomes the normal state.

Nobody is going to squeeze the admission from me that the so-so summer clothes I'm wearing don't bear the unmistakable air of last year. Nevertheless they always were good clothes, and I'm hanging on to them as long as they hang on to me.

Values change as swiftly and relentlessly as the war news. Things which once seemed as necessary as breathing are suddenly as unnecessary as goloshes in the sun. I would rather have goloshes in the sun than some of the goods which are listed as luxuries by the Government. In the new order of things, I'm going to have them always, anyway.

Items like lipsticks, brassières are sent me and all right with me, if you like, but peace — I mean, in this bag I dare say, lipstick — fancy things, of mother of pearl, jet, ivory, coral, shells, jade, and lapis lazuli, especially which have never been so much the necessities but luxuries of the heroines.

"If it is a question of one Government controlled luxury or another, I'll take a little piece of bird-cage wire."

...of my own.

In tortuous months, I've pulled to make the office cash box and office boys meet, left me for the warmest you-so-ers". "Must get-as-much-want" men? (around.)

Unfortunately! uncontrolled.

Meanwhile, if I can give his 70/- collection of fan-mail Cross Fund for every man, woman in this fair land the luxury of paper-we...

As for book-sifters, gymnasium appliances...

COOKERY

BECAUSE of its value...

LOVERS' CORNER.—Life is new and strange and wonderful to me. Last week, after three years' courtship, we became engaged. After all these years of uncertainty, I am content at last. Now I know that his love for me is as great as mine for him. I am rushing about from place to place, buying new dresses, and arranging this and that. I am just one out of a...

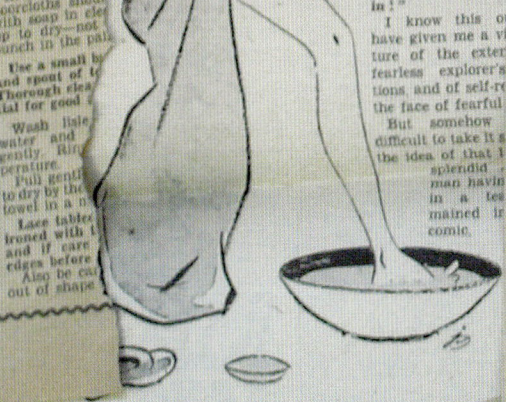

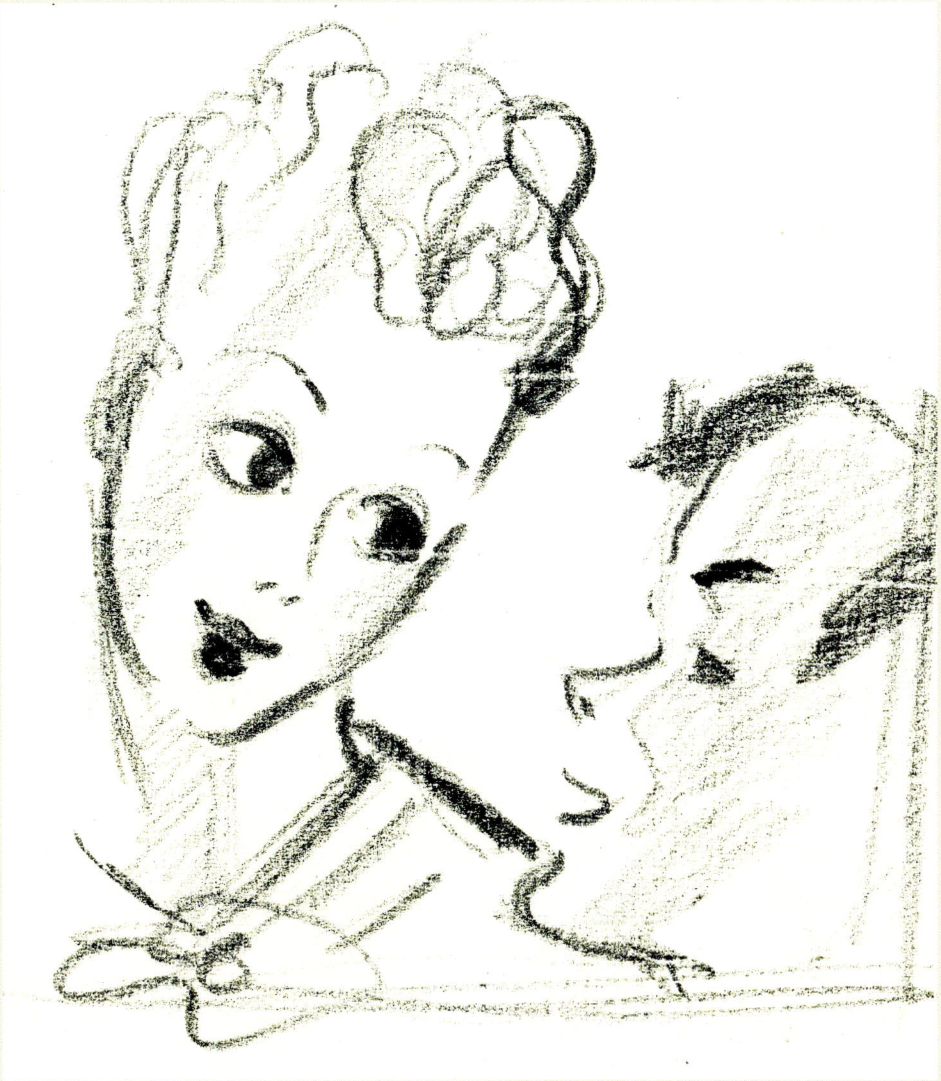

DESIGN DOSSIER

Line and wash drawing by Joy Batchelor.

Halas Batchelor

HALAS and Batchelor are a three-year-old partnership, and between them they cover the advertising front: Hallas designs mainly posters and direct mail, Bachelor press and direct mail also.

John Halas, Hungarian, is twenty-seven; Joy Batchelor twenty-four. When first they went into partnership, they were engaged in the production of advertising cartoon films, but, during the last year, have added posters, press work and direct mail to their repertoire; these latter now occupy them almost exclusively.

They left England to work in Budapest and Paris, and have been back in London only since July of last year. Returning, and faced with the difficulty of getting anyone to look at their work—much less to use it—Halas and Batchelor had the sort of lean time that reads well in biographies but tends to be less romantic for the actual duration. At this point, however, their individual biography merges into one that is almost common property among able but struggling young freelances in Britain: London Transport and Shell-Mex saw and used their work.

Lithography and letterpress are infectious: what was ignored or unseen as an original was noticed as a reproduction, and Halas and Batchelor are now finding an increasing market for their work.

Page from *Art and Industry*, fashion and advertising work. Most of the article deals with John's airbrushed posters.

Line drawing for *Harpers*. Smoking in the 1940s and 1950s was still seen as a sexy and attractive activity. If you look closely at the photos of Joy in this book it will be hard to find one in which she is not holding a cigarette.

49

Poor John is very sad, his wife is not too pretty but very clever, she is a secret witch, she can make all sorts of things happen, a lovely house, surrounded by a beautiful garden, all full of strawberries, pears, apric[ot]

When Joy and John Halas returned to England in 1938 they quickly became engaged in searching for work as commercial artists. One of the earliest examples of Joy's designs in 1939 is for a silk scarf decorated with the lyrics from Harry Bidgood's song *Run, Rabbit, Run*. The fluidity of the illustrations and design echo the energy and rhythm of the song. This is in contrast to the more personal drawings and cartoons that Joy produced about her relationship with John in Budapest in the spring of 1938. These light linear pencil drawings are proto-forms of illustrated motifs and forms Joy later produced for Josephine Terry's range of cookery books.

These sketches above, drawn in a light-hearted moment in Budapest, represent Joy's ability to mediate between different languages and cultures. It also presents Joy and John's personal vision and expression that brings to light the closeness of their creative relationship.

The overly domestic tone belies a more serious aspect to their relationship, in particular, the balancing of their creative work that was often dependent on a shared visual, rather than a verbal language. It is significant that on their return to Britain Joy became the driving force at the heart of the partnership. She frequently functioned as a communicative conduit and cultural interpreter between both cultures and clients, and this continued throughout the early years of their creative partnership in Britain.

Their creative partnership was cemented when they became part of J Walter Thompson advertising agency, where Joy's career reconnected with animation. While they continued to produce some commercial art' many of their commissions were for animated content. It could be argued that this was a natural course for the animated energy of her illustrations. Joy's strength lay in being able to mediate information into visual forms that the viewer processed and absorbed into new knowledge. Her designs and storyboards for the Ministry of Information and the Central Office of Information films draw on the skills of an illustrator rather than an animator. This highlights the significance of World War Two information films - that of direct and clear communication aimed at mediating between different groups. Joy ensured that there was a collective understanding of the reasoning behind any presentation.

This had its foundation in Joy's early career and in her formative art education at Watford

...rants, a lovely lake, good wine, sunshine, beautiful moon and stars, no aircraft noise, in the small house there will be books and everything you need, a more than sensational car to motor where you like. Yippee!

School of Art. Here, Joy learnt that the role of the illustrator was in part to displace their sense of self-expression in order to reflect the project in relation to the needs and desires of the client. As George Him states: 'If we call ourselves designers it is only to stress that we are artists in the old sense, in that we are prepared to subordinate our personal aim – which, as for all creative people is self-expression – to the task we are given; and we believe that both can be compatible.' (Him, cited Artmonsky, 2012)

Significantly, Joy had a sense of independence and strength during a period in which women were starting to have more freedom. In particular women artists like Enid Marx, Margaret Calkin James, Betty Swanwick and Pearl Falconer were able to develop careers, most notably producing commercial art, including posters for London Transport and London Underground. The diversity of their commercial practice included textile design, book covers and other printed ephemeral, contributing and enriching the visual culture of contemporary Britain. Others such as Pearl Binder produced work that documented the richness and diversity of different communities of Britain, in particular the East End of London.

Unfortunately the ephemeral nature of the commercial illustration work produced from the early 1900s has mostly not survived and that which has survived lacks accreditation for the artists. Cheryl Buckley argues that: 'Women's interventions, both past and present, are consistently ignored. Indeed, the omissions are so overwhelming, and the rare acknowledgment so cursory and marginalized, that one realizes these silences are not accidental and haphazard; rather, they are the direct consequence of specific historiographic methods.' (Buckley 1986:3)

As Linda Nochlin (1971) and Cheryl Buckley (1986) have commented, women artists remain historically absent from the discourse of art and design production and criticism. Joy and many other female illustrators remain unaccredited, unrepresented and not discussed in relation to their contribution to our visual culture. This in part reflects the social dynamics of the period, in which limited credit was given to freelancer commercial artists, to the extent that even those that came to the forefront after much struggle, were soon forgotten by subsequent generations.

As noted elsewhere, Joy is often associated with her husband John Halas to the extent that Joy's

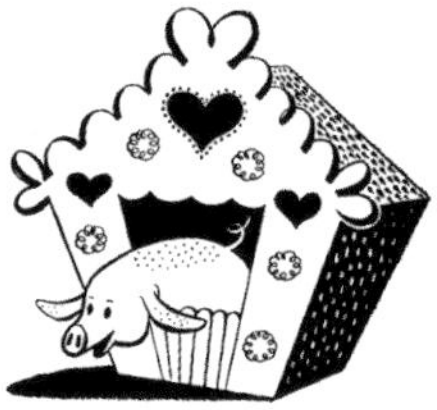

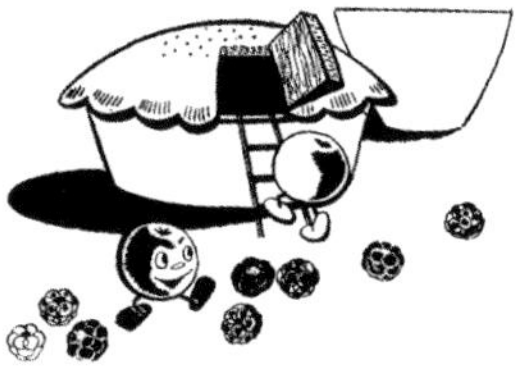

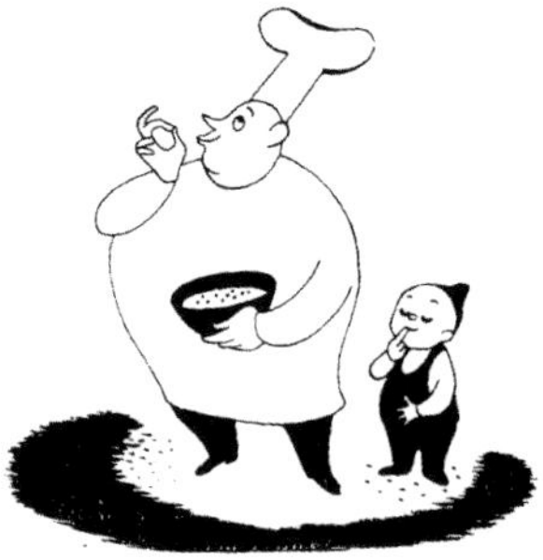

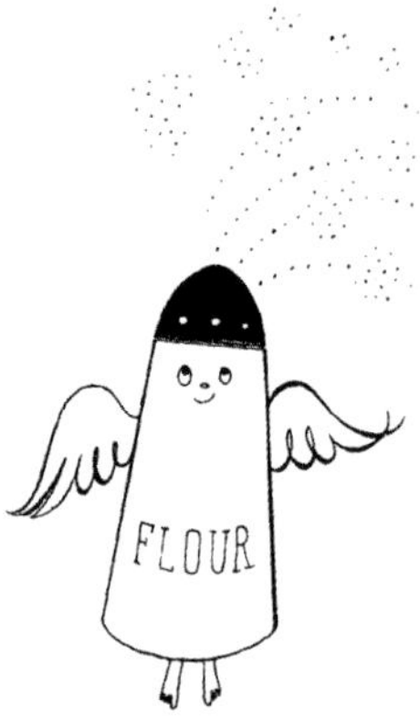
FLOUR

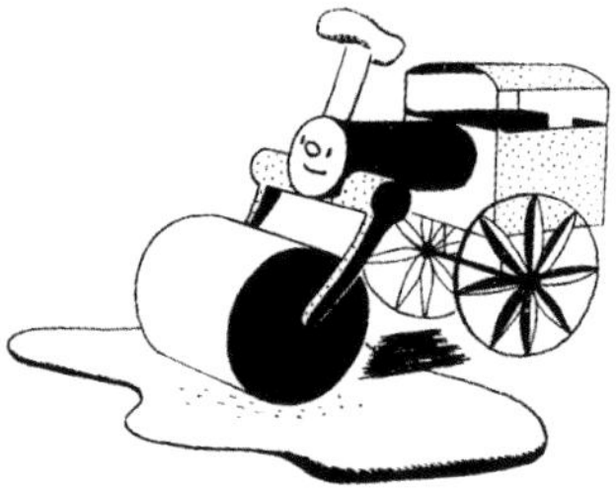

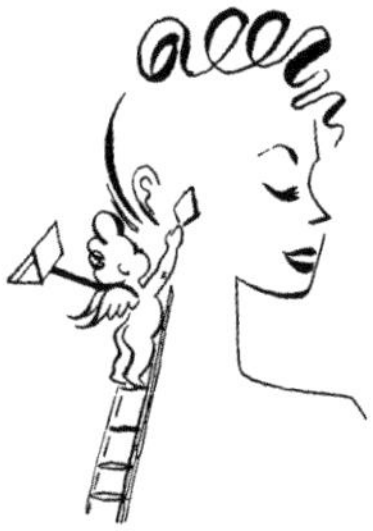

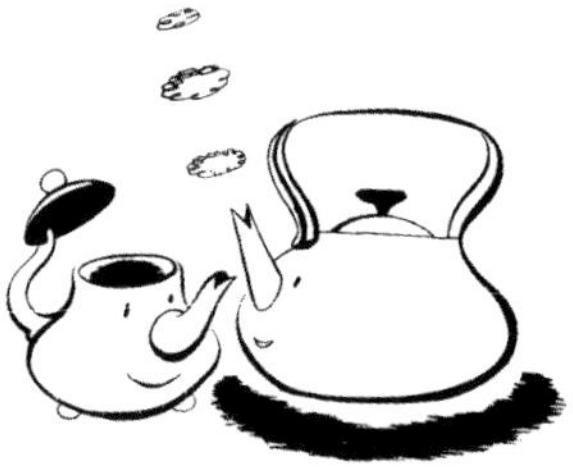

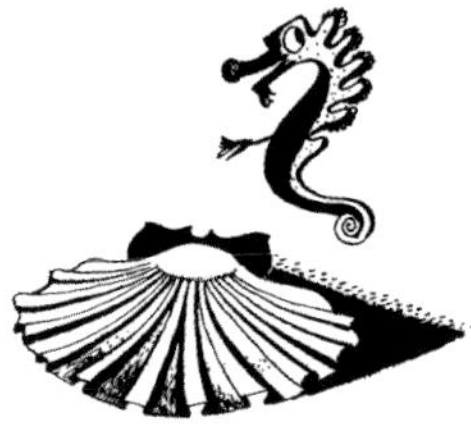

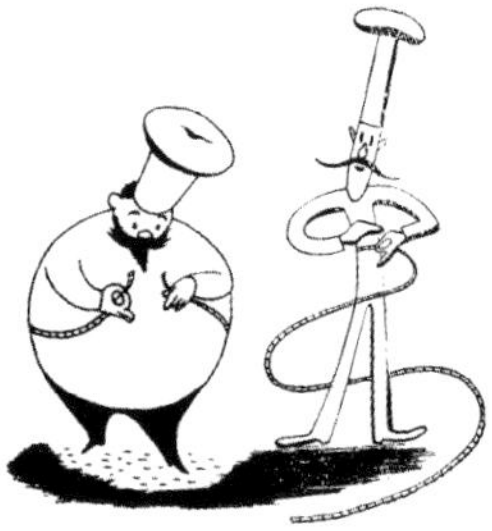

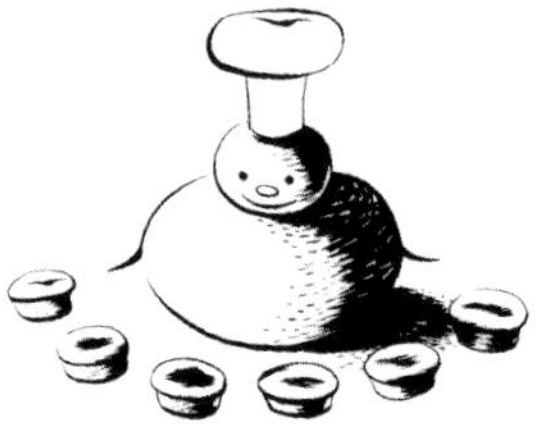

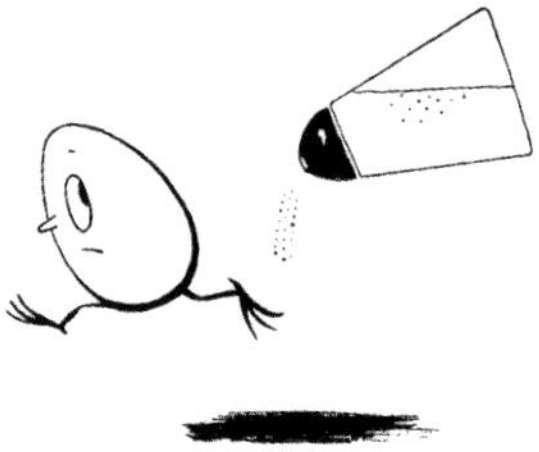

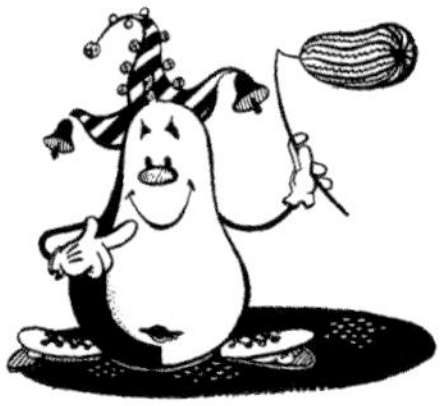

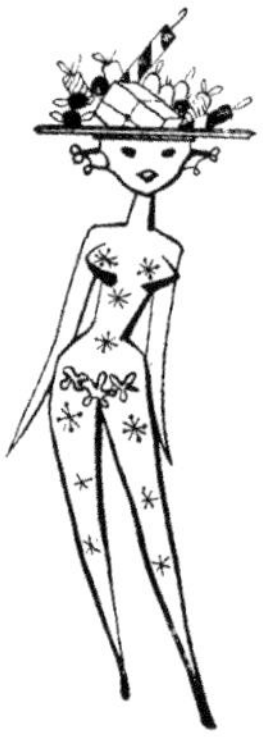

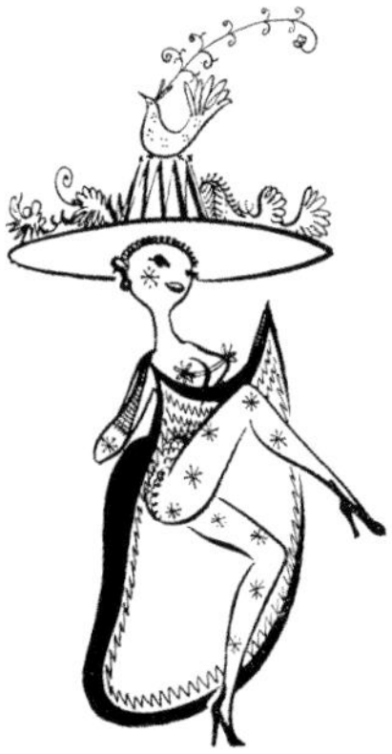

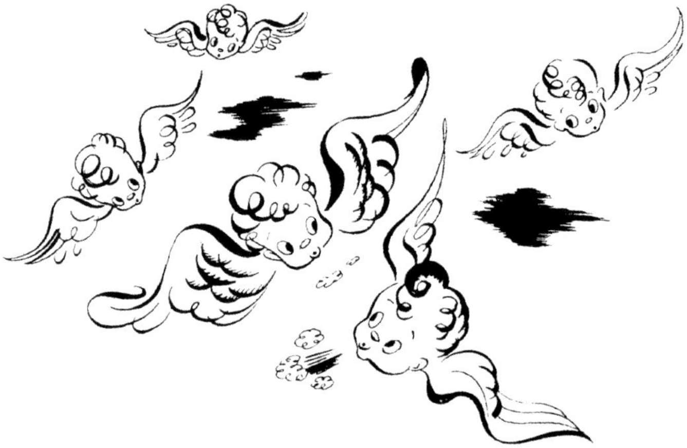

creative output and creative practice is often seen as less important. This remains a constant issue in terms of evaluating her work, yet her ability to mediate between different creative, social and domestic demands is ever present. Even when critics and reviewers discuss her work, there is a distinctive bias. When the creative partnership between Joy and John is discussed they dwell on gender, marriage and domestic life rather than Joy's artistic practice, even though it stands out and demands attention. In an article in *Art and Industry Magazine* it states that 'Joy Batchelor's line sketches have an attractive sparkle and slickness of line; they have been used by such magazines as *The Queen*. She has also done folders for the GPO which demonstrate an aptitude for clarity of layout and presentation.' Yet most of the article is given over to John, supported by a larger amount of visual examples of his commercial illustrations.

The unbalanced representation of Joy's work and creative contribution was sustained in the 1950s during the promotion of the production of *Animal Farm*. Photographs of Joy situate her in domestic settings that simultaneously represent her as a mother, wife, and animator/illustrator, reinforced by the presence of Vivien and Paul. A motif of domestic life is also used in promotional photographs of Joy with a character model of Charley for the series of films. In contrast to this domestic narrative it is suggested that Joy's ability to mediate opposing narratives and worlds is evident in her book illustrations for *Animal Farm*. In particular the pastel landscape romance, and fractured spaces found in Ravilious and Bawden are scraped away in *Animal Farm*. While the panoramic landscape is evoked, there is a dramatic and stark cut in this illusionary fabric that foregrounds the displacement of the pigs from the land. Joy expresses this through differences in horizontal and vertical compositions and lines. It is not as brutal as Paul Hogarth's 1966 illustrations for the cover of Penguin Book's version of *Animal Farm*, but it avoids the brightness and some of the sweetness that pervades elements of the animal designs and mise-en-scene of the animated feature. While this was the only novel that Joy illustrated, and illustrators are often defined by the books they illustrate, it remains an example of her ability to bring to life the text of the author through the mediation of her imagination and vision. As Joseph Pennell noted: 'The illustrator - the real illustrator - is an artist who can show what the author meant to say and couldn't - an artist who can make something out of his author.' (Pennell, 1913: p.25-26)

Pen and ink illustrations by Joy for various cookery books by Josephine Terry and Muriel Goaman in 1950 and 1952 (previous page).

Illustrations from *The Truth About Stork* by Edward Fyfe Griffith 1948 (this page).

54

The two results expected of this film are assumed to be:-

a) reminder value - restating lessons in health precaution already learned.

b) humour value - easing the irksomeness of the precautions by associating them with an entertaining cartoon.

The formula suggested to give a dramatic shape to episodes without any inherent crescendo is that of the Ten Little Nigger Boys or, in this case, the Six little Tommies. Malaria - then there were five: Scrub-Typhus - then there were four: V.D. - then there were three, and so on until only Tommy Atkins, who took all the recommended precautions, is left. Single handed he accomplishes his mission, and gets his due reward - (The V.C.) watched enviously by the five hospital cases and suitably acclaimed and fussed over not only by the girl he left behind him but by the five little sweethearts of the five defaulters.

Halas Batchelor CARTOON FILM UNIT

TITLE "HEALTH IN JUNGLE WARFARE"

These pencil illustrations by Joy were used as a style guide for *Six Little Jungle Boys* (1945). She and John worked closely together on this film, that was started in 1943 titled *Jungle Warfare*, as can be seen above on the film label. Next to it is the very proscriptive brief from the Ministry of Information.

It was these kinds of projects that diverted Joy's potential as an artist to the more diverse activities of getting across information to an audience in subjects that were often challenging.

A personal sketch made in Ross on Wye. Vivien remembers, 'This was framed and in my bedroom when I was a child. I always thought it looked like a hedgehog'.

An illustration for the *Daily Mirror*, 1940.

Pen and ink drawing for the illustrated version of *Animal Farm* (1954), published by Secker and Warburg.

References:
Artmonsky, Ruth (2013) *Designing Women: Women Working in Advertising and Publicity from the 1920s to the 1960s* London: Artmonsky Arts
Buckley, Cheryl (1986) 'Made in Patriarchy': Towards a Feminist Analysis of Women and Design: *Design Issues* Vol.3 No.2, p.3-14
Cubitt, Sean (2005) *The Cinema Effect* Cambridge, Massachusetts: MIT Press
Longman, Grant 'School of Art in South West Hertfordshire 1800-1950' in Jones-Baker, Doris (ed) (2004) *Hertfordshire in History* Hatfield: Hertfordshire Publications p.237-246
Nochlin, Linda (1971) 'Why Have There Been No Great Women Artists?' *ARTnews* 69, 9 January 1971, pp.22-39, p.67-7
Pennell, Joseph 'The Coming Illustration' *The Imprint*, January 1913 p.25-26

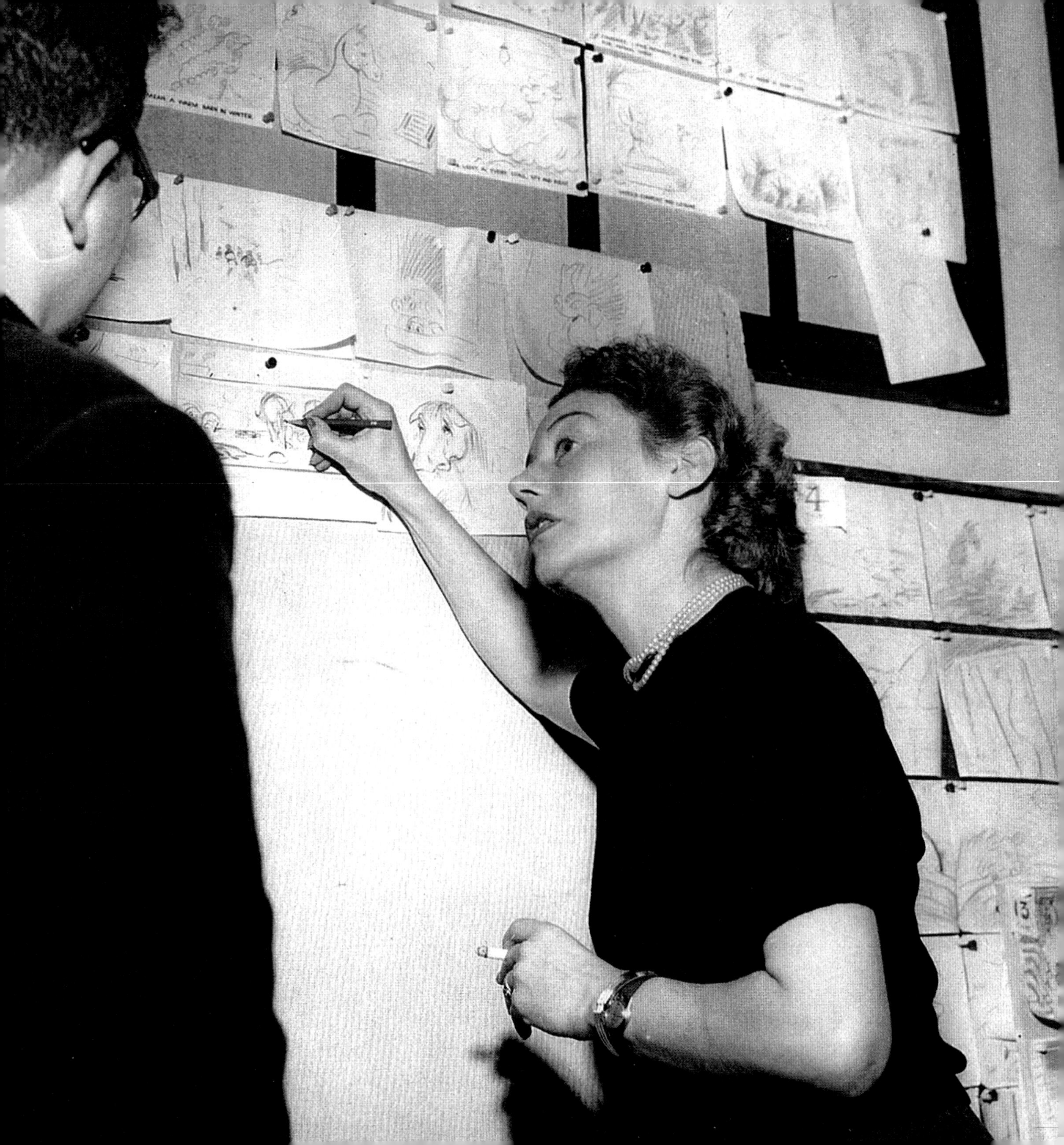
4

Joy, Britain Needs You *Paul Wells*

It is now customary for specific authors to situate themselves in regard to the subjects they write about. I should declare then that my initial interest in the 'Halas & Batchelor' project (as it might be termed) was kindled by the small fact that I shared a birthday with Joy Batchelor, May 12th, and this intrigued me to know who she was, and what she did. Little did I know, then, that much later I would embark on extensive research lasting over a twenty-year period in which I would discover the Halas & Batchelor studio, write about some of its wartime shorts, co-write a history-cum-critical analysis of *Halas & Batchelor Cartoons* with Vivien Halas, the daughter of John and Joy, and thereafter, make a documentary, recovering the still largely uncelebrated innovation and prescience of John Halas.

There was good reason for all of this. Even now it seems bizarre that so few people have heard of a studio that existed from 1940 to 1995, in near constant production, and which almost singularly defined British animation until the emergence of Aardman.

Joy working on the first layouts for the pre-production of *Animal Farm* that took a year to prepare. The paper storyboard filled two rooms of their studio in Paddington.

ASIFA meeting in Annecy, 1960. From left to right: Raymond Maillet and possibly his wife, Paul Grimault, John Halas, Pierre Barban and Joy Batchelor.

Yet more absurd that no one outside the animation industry - globally - really knows who John Halas is, when he did so much to progress animation as a form creatively, aesthetically, technologically, commercially and intellectually, on a world stage, and when animation played an important role in a dialogue with social and political affairs. His role in the ASIFA (Association Internationale du Film d'Animation) organisation, for example, cannot be understated, in that he was clearly instrumental in bringing together the world's animators into an extended conversation with each other, and in regard to the importance of their art as a vehicle for quasi-utopian thought and aesthetics. So, now in 2014, as contemporary culture starts to define and trace the impact of Fourth-Wave Feminism, and take stock of the social-media-led, web-enhanced information era, it is surely time to properly recover and address the figure of Joy Batchelor. Though often seen in his shadow, Joy was Halas's marital, creative and business partner, and herself a pioneering woman (socially and professionally), and one of the key developers of modes of 'visual communication', or in her terms, 'communications design', in the industrial and educational form.

The year 1914, of course, is incontrovertibly the touchstone for the beginning of a re-appraisal of the modern world with the outbreak of World War One. This somewhat obscures and diminishes some more locally significant acts that provide useful touchstones for this discussion. In March 1914, for example, suffragette Mary Richardson decided to storm into the National Gallery in London, and take a meat cleaver to Velázquez's painting, *Rokeby Venus*, presumably as an act of protest about its possibly salacious and erotic representation of female vanity. It was not the only challenging development in the art world that year, as Wyndham Lewis launched the influential *Blast* magazine, announcing the progressive intentions of Vorticism, while Umberto Boccioni published on the technical and aesthetic innovation of Futurism, an exhibition of works later taking place at the Dore Gallery. The London Group, featuring established female artists like Ethel Sands, and her partner, Anna Hope 'Nan' Hudson, also held its first exhibition, and *London Opinion* graced its cover with Alfred Leete's now seminal poster of Lord Kitchener, asserting that 'Your Country Needs You'. 1914 was also the year that Joy Batchelor was born.

If Richardson's act marks the near-end of the First-Wave of feminism as women moved towards securing the vote, if modernist manifestos started to re-define what art could do and achieve, and if World War One prompted the first key developments in mass communication design, it is clear that the creative agenda was being re-set in re-positioning the way in which a changing Britain might be understood. It is these core themes - the social and professional place of women; the shifts in modern mass media communications; and new models of creative endeavour - which were to be the ongoing backdrop to Batchelor's life and career.

When Virginia Woolf gave the lectures in 1929 that would ultimately form the text of *A Room of One's Own*, she spoke in a spirit that sought to enhance the place of women socially and culturally, following on from the legal and political enfranchisement achieved by securing the vote. She stressed that for a woman to be a successful writer she required an education, economic security and her own space to create. The book was embraced as a feminist text, only much later by Second-Wave Feminists, who essentially emerged in the mid-1960s, only to acknowledge that despite achieving democratic rights and principles, women had yet to really challenge the social inequalities embedded in lived experience.

The period, then, between the late-1920s and the early 1960s, works as a time in which, on the one hand, during the war periods, women were advantaged by being conspicuous parts of the workforce, while still retaining their traditional role as domestic carers, while on the other, they were demoted and marginalized in the post-war period as men became socially privileged in 'reward' for their war service. Though this might seem a little too simplistic and generalised, there are distinct echoes of this paradigm in the flux of identity and status that Batchelor was to endure, in what might be termed the 'lost years' of formally feminist social intervention.

Woolf's suggestion that a woman must have an education found purchase in Batchelor's successful time at the Watford School of Art, but the lack of economic security prevented her taking up a scholarship at the Slade school, her family insisting she find work. Her first job was as an in-betweener at Dennis Connelly's animation studio, seemingly a long way from 'a room of her own'. Nevertheless, Batchelor was part of the initial personnel participating in the first attempts to set up an inevitably flawed Taylorist-style production line, perfected at Disney, which ostensibly saw studios as potential animation 'factories', where women played crucial, if seemingly easily dismissed roles in the animation process, from mixing the paint to animating short sequences. As Clare Kitson notes in her essay in this volume, this was an incipient moment of small-scale empowerment for women, which in Batchelor's case ultimately manifested itself in the evolution of a high quality, predominantly female production team at Halas & Batchelor, including Vera Linnecar, Rosalie (Wally) Crook and Kathleen (Spud) Houston.

Crucially, though, in the early years, it was

A cel from *Animal Farm* showing 'the chickens revolt'. They were promised that their eggs would never be taken.

Batchelor's skill with language that proved to be the core of her own development in this period. Though she became a competent animator, and it enabled her to work with Halas on *Music Man* (1938), the first Technicolor cartoon completed in England, it was her major skills in speaking, writing and illustrating that enabled her to represent herself, Halas (a Hungarian with a limited grasp of English), and ultimately, the company they founded in 1940, in addressing a range of possible clients and customers. This should not be under estimated since, as Batchelor recalled, John's command of English was limited: 'We conversed through the media of pencil and paper, signs and gestures and some form of ESP. It worked pretty well.' Even these early models of exchange, then, signal Batchelor's command of a visual literacy which was a key currency in her creative career.

Though Woolf may have meant a 'room of one's own' in a more rarified sense of a place to write literary forms, Batchelor - herself a devotee of classical literature - soon understood that she possessed a key skill in articulating ideas in conceptual and visual terms, and further how this was a distinctive aspect of the evolving language of animation. Inevitably, in this period, though, her personal circumstances in shortly becoming one of the first vanguard of working mothers necessitated that the studio and her home became her creative 'room'. Even in this, though, Batchelor is a notable role model for women, given her level of productivity and success while ensuring that her two children enjoyed their upbringing (see Vivien Halas's recollections in this volume). As Batchelor noted, 'One of the big tests of a marriage/work relationship is the recognition of the need for constant adjustment to changing circumstances - and it can be painful. However, much as I missed the daily drama of working with John Halas and the group in the studio, the immense reward of being a mother and still being able to contribute, in a different way, to the work of the studio was unbelievably fortunate.' Again, it is important to stress here, that though Batchelor was an established public figure, it was both her status as a woman in a still largely patriarchal and male-centred world, and her very adaptability in responding to 'changing circumstances', that undermined, and to a certain extent compromised, her professional identity and presence.

It is important to recall then that Batchelor's role was especially significant in that initially, and over time, she had to convince possible sponsors and financiers of the usefulness of animation in delivering abstract concepts and metaphors to sell goods and market services, at a time when animation was unproven in Britain as a visual communications form per se. (European companies already frequently used animated commercials to advertise their wares.) Equally, she had to use her knowledge of England and the English, to facilitate ways in which the Eastern European aesthetics so favoured by Halas might be made acceptable to, and effective for, British companies and audiences. As Hediger and Vonderau have pointed out, though, the kinds of industrial, utility and public information films

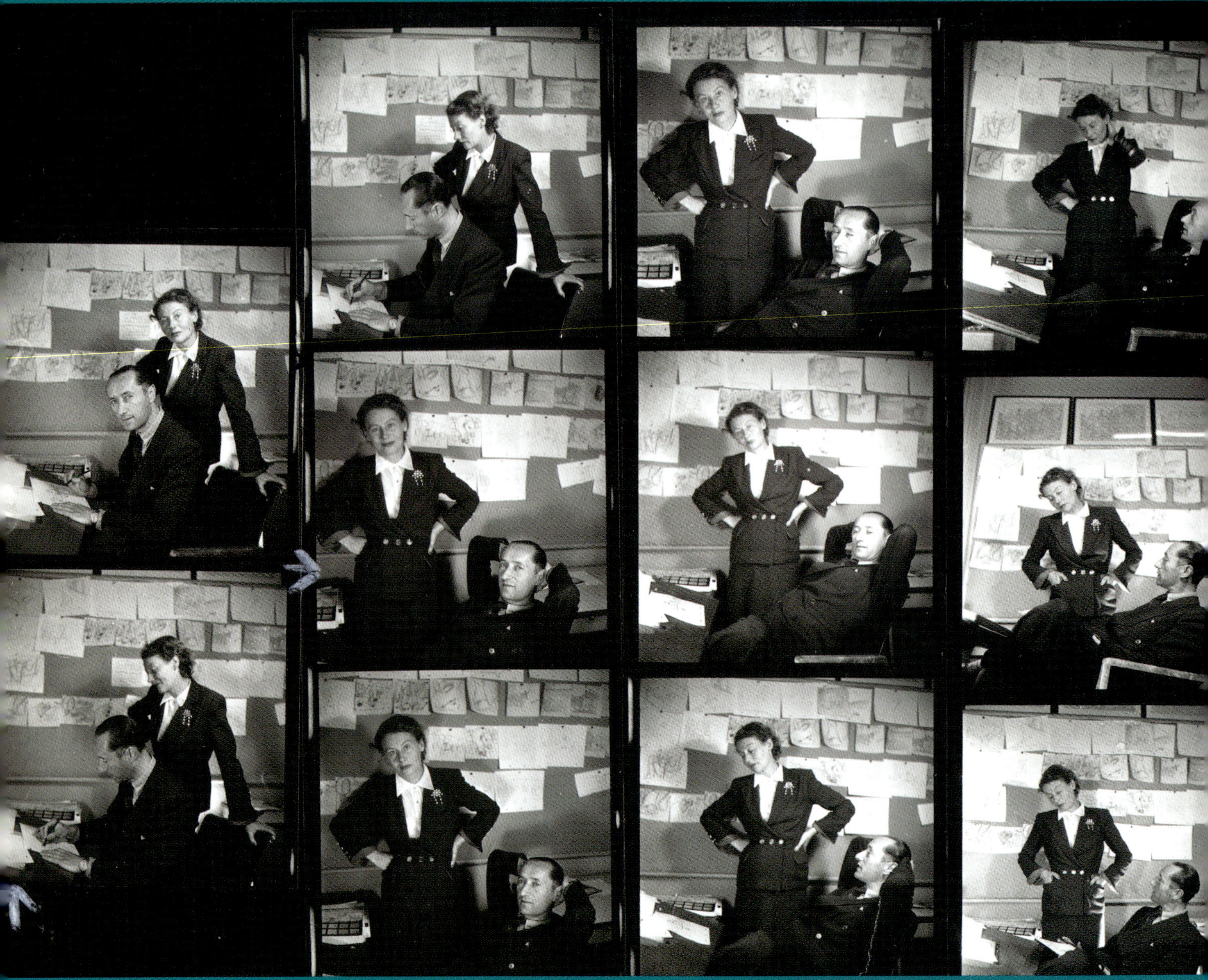

Halas & Batchelor were to make 'cannot be divorced from the conditions of their production and the contexts of their use. Far from constituting self-sufficient entities for aesthetic analysis [these] films have to be understood in terms of their specific, usually organizational, purpose, and in the very context of power and organizational practice in which they appear.' (Hediger & Vonderau (eds) 2009:10) The work the studio undertook then for J Walter Thompson, the Ministry of Information, the Central Office of Information and numerous other sponsors, thereafter, was inextricably bound up with the identity and message of the funding body in the historical moment of production and exhibition, and not the identity of the studio, and even less its individual creative talents.

Further, and crucially, Elsaesser insists that the fact that such films have *auftrag* (an occasion), *anlass* (a purpose) and *adressat* (an addressee), and not an auteur (see Hediger & Vonderau (eds)19-34) compromises the acknowledgment of any creative achievement in the work. Almost at the very outset, then, Batchelor - already made less 'visible' socially at one level, through her status as a woman and as someone engaged in what would later be termed 'multitasking' - was working in a form that was not subject to praise for its potential aesthetic qualities, nor for its authorship. It should be noted that there is little doubt that Halas very much had the ambition to be acknowledged as an artist and as an authorial figure, and his more progressive projects readily signal this. Batchelor, though, for all her obvious 'authorship', both in script and design, was essentially denied acknowledgement by the established principle that industrial, utility, educational and public information forms were concerned with their message and audience first and foremost. Equally, such films - even if beautiful and effective in their moment of production - were intrinsically ephemeral. Any academic intervention to more properly claim 'authorship' in these films, thereafter, has been essentially absent, and has also long since been overtaken by the desire to place such films in critical contexts that suggest that they better represent and evidence 'record (institutional memory), rhetoric (governance) and rationalization (optimizing process)'. (Hediger & Vonderau (eds) 2009:11) From the perspective of this discussion, it is important then to recover Batchelor as a deviser, writer and image maker in the service of these issues, but also, to recover her authorship and aesthetic outlook.

At the point when World War Two broke out, and Halas was threatened with internment on the Isle of Man as an 'enemy alien', Batchelor married him, in turn becoming a 'friendly enemy alien' herself. There is some irony, then, in the fact that the very same government that harboured wartime suspicions of the émigré Halas, ultimately commissioned the studio to do public information film work on its behalf.

Batchelor was later to note, 'As bombs showered over London during the early years of the war, the British Ministry of Information turned to two young animators to assist with essential information about how to survive the war.

Films were made about growing your own vegetables, saving paper, metal and bones for the war effort and how to protect yourself from enemy spies. We produced 70 propaganda films between 1940 and 1944 with a very small unit working to the point of total exhaustion, under the most difficult of circumstances; shortage of paper, pencils, film stock and cel materials.' (Quoted in Halas & Wells 2006:90)

Batchelor's pragmatism in the circumstances – another uncelebrated but essential personal and professional quality – also informed her understanding that the discourse of these types of films had to necessarily be translated into social practice. This required a particular understanding of the precise execution of briefs; the importance of research and the ways it informed possible narratives and design outlooks; the clear representation of strategic and procedural methods; the fundamental limits on production imposed by economy and time; and the profound importance of knowing the audience.

These became the key principles in the soon evolving discipline of 'visual communication'. It is right and proper then to suggest that Batchelor, certainly within the British context, was a pioneering figure in evolving methods and processes by which to make effective animated films in this ephemeral but nevertheless socially vital sub-genre of practice.

Batchelor's resourcefulness and ability to improvise were important factors in this work, thereafter.

An early *Animal Farm* script with corrections by Joy.

In many of her projects she became an inveterate problem solver, but more importantly, determined particular strategies by which she could use animation as a visual communications tool to demonstrate approaches to problems and to offer solutions. Though she co-authored many scripts during the war period, her first outstanding solo script was for *Modern Guide to Health* (1946). Made for the COI, and the Ministry of Health in support of the National Health Service, it counselled on general health awareness, and included some of Batchelor's signature motifs:

• an advisory voiceover exercising a playful tension between the ignorance of the subject (the audience) and the role of the expert;

• simplified graphics in the service of making clear points using memorable and iconic imagery;

• the use of penetration (the depiction of interior organic, mechanical or psychological states not available to the naked eye and hard to imagine);

• using key symbolic contrasts between comparative situations and environments;

• and crucially, having diagnosed and articulated a problem, offering a demonstrably positive outcome as a consequence of undertaking the suggested actions.

In this case, the film demonstrates better posture by showing a human figure as a moving skeleton, and shows the problems caused to feet by socks and shoes that are too small and crush the malleable bones of young children. People are advised to seek fresh air and sunshine at the weekends to escape the dirt and oppression of the workplace factories and the urban environment they experience during the week. There is also caution here, though, as a young woman is advised to protect herself from too much hot sun. Further, in the film's most striking imagery, a woman is revisited by the anxieties of her domestic tasks while she sleeps - a sewing needle stitches her bed, arousing her from her slumbers. Indeed, calm and relaxing sleep is shown to be illusory in relation to the oppressiveness and exhaustion of the constant cooking, cleaning, ironing, shopping etc, that characterises the woman's life. This sequence demonstrates Batchelor's increasing concerns for women, and is the first recognition that the war has not changed and advanced social conditions for women; indeed, it had potentially made them worse. In a seeming acceptance that there can be no easy or radical intervention, the woman is advised to relax for half an hour before she sleeps, and to not worry about things she cannot change.

Though there seems to be an implicit resignation in this in regard to its social comment on the immediate post-war period - a scepticism further advanced in the range of female stereotypes in *Dolly Put the Kettle On* (1947) - it is arguably the case that the studio's work should be understood less within an explicitly political context but as part of a wider, more progressive ideological and cultural paradigm. The film, like the innovatory *Charley* series (1948/49), *The Shoemaker and the*

Charley series 1948-49

Joy and John's work for the British government during World War Two enabled them to establish close links with the decision makers of the time, such as Sir Stafford Cripps, the Chancellor of the Exchequer, a key figure in the establishment of the Welfare State - something both Joy and John felt to be important. The introduction of the National Insurance Act in 1948 was an opportunity to hone their animation skills in producing this series of public information films to convey complex reforms in an engaging way, something that Joy became particularly good at.

Charley, scripted, directed and initially designed by Joy, was a recalcitrant 'everyman' figure who guided the audience through the new system. He grumpily objected to everything, rejecting change, before being shown how he would benefit and thus taking the audience with him in understanding and accepting the new National Insurance Act.

Hatter (1949), *The Figurehead* (1953) and *For Better, For Worse* (1961) – all with scripts specifically by Batchelor – is situated at the juncture between what Elsaessar sees as two different kinds of modernism. These were: 'an avant garde high-art modernism, of revolt and revolution, and an avant garde of industrial modernism or commercial modernism, of advertising and design, serviced more by filmic modes modelled on industrial films than experimental style or formally innovative technique.' (Hediger & Vonderau (eds) 2009:22) It is clear that Halas was striving for the former modernist mode, while Batchelor became invested in the latter; the couple ultimately used animation to revise, refresh and combine avant garde approaches in both kinds of modernist practice.

To properly evaluate Batchelor's work as a director and scriptwriter, I wish to assess five different films that reveal her approach and her sustained engagement with the animation screenwriting process. Batchelor's skill in drawing upon modernist design aesthetics while speaking to commercial concerns is readily evidenced, for example, in *What's Cooking?* (1947), which deploys a script composed in rhyme in which vegetables, among them a talking aubergine, some geisha-style onions and some synchronised swimming carrots, seek out flavour in the shape of a jar of Bovril. A housewife stirs an enormous pot of stew, and any sense of the wartime era of austerity is forgotten as an everyday environment and ordinary foodstuffs are rendered exotic and playful – traditional beef stew made the stuff of collaboration and inspiration. The sheer quality of the animation wholly advances the form as a modernist form of expression, Batchelor embedding aesthetic innovation in the seemingly ordinary context of the domestic market place and not arts culture.

More significantly, in regard to the evolving conditions of visual communication and selling goods, Batchelor enables the transformation both of the material world – the vegetables take on anthropomorphic tendencies and processes of production – and the 'reality' of the brand. 'Bovril' in itself becomes transformative; it literally changes the world played out in the scenario, and in doing so advances its own status as a brand. These become the sophisticated conditions of commercial practice, and Batchelor, in little more than ten years of work, becomes one the most adept practitioners in the field.

Batchelor's skills were quickly evident and frequently practised, enabling her to use different techniques and approaches dependent upon the project involved and the outcome desired.

Her understanding of what commercial clients required was astute, seeing her work in a way that drew emphatic attention to the product at the conclusion of a commercial by ensuring that a visually and textually playful opening narrative entertained the viewer rather than simply instilling a didactic message. This was especially important not merely in the context of advertising but in more ideologically-charged films, and most particularly her work on the studio's masterpiece, *Animal Farm* (1954).

It is here perhaps that it is possible to properly acknowledge Batchelor's quality as a writer. As Batchelor noted, 'While I had learnt by trial and error to write, plan and storyboard films, John Halas had learnt more about how to organise, train and generate enthusiasm in people, and he proceeded to lay down the master plan for reorganising the studio while I made a master plan for the script.' Batchelor's approach to adaptation was predicated on making sure that the film properly embraced Orwell's fable in order to make a serious animated feature, simultaneously revising the by-this-time embedded view that animated features were funny animal stories.

Arguably, Batchelor found a Woolfian 'room of her own' by ensuring that she wrote in a spirit that played out the 'close integration [of] the essential design discipline [with] those of drama, ballet and mime together with social and literary studies [and] allied to graphics and photography'. These were the essential aspects that she saw not merely in animation but as central to visual literacy and communication.

In Batchelor's scripts, her scene descriptors and voiceover/dialogue, allied to her visual sense as a graphic designer, combine effectively to properly exploit what she believed animation could distinctively offer. She suggests 'the great strength of animation lies in its power to make literal what is normally figurative, in its power of exaggeration in order to present ideas with impact, its ability to project a thought until it obtains an entirely new and more truthful aspect.' Her attention to detail is clear in these respects, evidenced, for example here, in Sequence One from the Fifth draft of *Animal Farm*:

1 It is evening in midsummer. The sun is setting. The opening view shows from high up a number of farms in various stages of development. A village and the village inn - The Red Lion - are also visible. It will be absolutely clear in the establishing scene that Manor Farm is the worst kept farm in the area, and that, with the exception of Frederic's farm, the other farms look prosperous and well kept.
2 The final panning shot ends on the entrance to Manor Farm, showing the notice board. The Raven is perched on top. He looks in direction (sic) of food store and flies off.
3 Track into lighted lantern outside food store. (Jones's figure is hidden by angle of wall). Following scenes are carried by sound effects.

4 Cut to close up of lantern light flickering in draught. Hear offstage noises of key being turned in padlock.
5 Cut to close up of Jones's hands in lantern light as he finishes key turning. The padlock is left swinging.
6 Hand picks up lantern. We hear Jones's feet crunching on cobbled yard.
7 Follow feet as Jones lurches alongside barn. Frightened mice scurry out from an old tin. Jones flattens the tin under his boot as he stumbles along.
8 Light from lantern falls on chicken house.
9 Inside, roosting hens crouch back apprehensively as the light shines in.
10 Outside, the hencoop door is kicked shut, but it is old and swings open again as Jones goes off.
11 Cows from within their stalls cringe back from lantern light as Jones is heard continuing his round of the yard.
12 We see his feet and the lantern approaching.
13 From their jointly shared stall, Boxer and Benjamin look out apprehensively. They duck back as the stable door is slammed on them to reveal Jones's face (for first time). As he comes forward out of screen the stable door also creaks back to show Boxer and Benjamin peering out of the crack.
14 Cut to bottle as Jones raises it to drink. He wipes his mouth and comes forward.
15 Cut to pigs watching him from sty.
16 Jones drunkenly approaches back door of farmhouse in long shot.
17 We see him closer as he nears the door. Jessie the dog slinks off at his approach. Pan with her.
18 Cut to Jones hurling the now empty bottle at her. Bottle crashes. Jessie shoots off howling.
19 Back to door as Jones disappears inside. Light appears inside kitchen window.
20 From inside their sty the pigs watch the lighted window. From inside stall Boxer and Benjamin look at it too.
21 Cows watch from the stable. Track into towards house as the light goes from kitchen to bedroom and finally goes out.

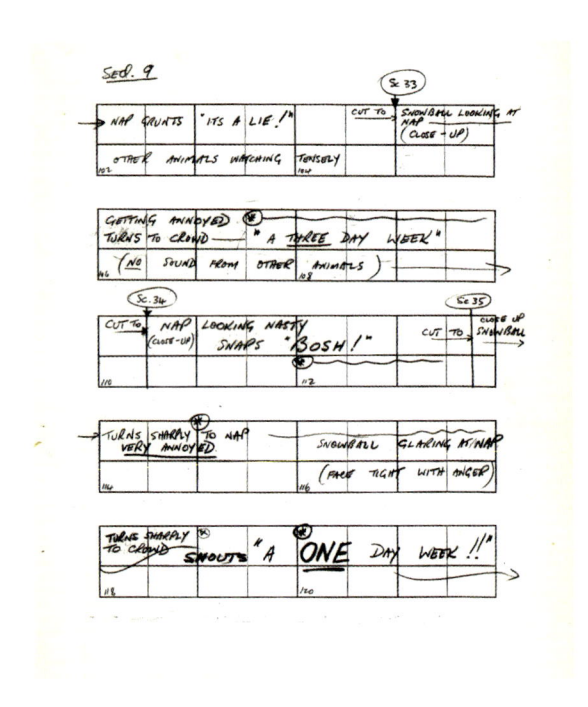

An *Animal Farm* worksheet, with music effects and imagery linked and precisely charted.

It is noticeable that Batchelor is concerned here to not merely establish a context, but to create a mood and atmosphere, and to prefigure the symbolic character tensions that emerge later in the film. Intrinsic to this is her use of the shifting dynamics of the light to dramatise the introduction of the environment, the conditions and implied attitude of the animals, and the small but affecting actions taking place in the dark. Jones is a threatening presence, his demeanour suggested through sounds, the slamming of the stable door, his crushing of the tin can and the breaking of the bottle. There is nothing here of slapstick idioms,

cute animals and primary colour palettes. Rather, there is literary sensitivity; social awareness; graphic qualities; drama suggested specifically through mime and motion; and the cinematic dynamics available in animation design and art direction. For *Animal Farm*, Batchelor also added to the arsenal of the animation scriptwriter by adding what she called a 'Tension Chart', articulating the film over a long stretch of paper. The chart included an unfolding storyline; a tension line noting the dramatic expectancy of the action and situation; guidelines in relation to mood and music; advice on the colour palette (anticipating contemporary colour scripts); and finally, time lines noting the seasons, time of day, etc. Having achieved this analytical breakdown, Batchelor could move through the script stage with greater confidence, knowing too, that the script would remain fluid and develop further as the storyboarding advanced.

This parallel development of script drafts and visualisation suited feature-length work, and both echoed practices at the Disney studio during the 1930s, and anticipated the ways in which studios like Pixar and Dreamworks work in the contemporary era. Once more, though it is easy to be distracted by other aspects of the success of *Animal Farm*, it is important to recall Batchelor's creative input and impact on what still remains a landmark animated feature. Batchelor preserves the literary quality of the piece while also ensuring that the distinctive credentials of animation are foregrounded in the service of mature storytelling and intellectual themes. These same skills were deployed in Batchelor's most singularly auteurist project, that of adapting Gilbert and Sullivan's 1887 opera, *Ruddigore* (1964).

Halas & Batchelor's 55-minute television film was the first opera to be adapted into an extended animation. Plans to re-work *The Mikado, Pirates of Penzance* and *HMS Pinafore* were rejected by the D'Oyly Carte Opera Company, on the basis that the notoriously particular and purist Gilbert and Sullivan audience would not be able to accept these classics in abridged form. Even *Ruddigore,* though less commercially successful than the other operas, was a risk. This was reflected in a problematic production process, subject to many delays, in which the musical and narrative continuity became subject to constant revision. *Ruddigore*, also known as *The Witch's Curse,* was Gilbert and Sullivan's tenth collaboration, opening at the Savoy Theatre in 1887, and running for 288 performances. In typically witty style, Gilbert parodies melodramatic conventions making heroes less than heroic, villains more than successful, and a happy ending subject to many compromises.

By the time it was made as an animation in the mid-1960s, Batchelor ensured it echoed the more ambiguous moral and social climate of the era, and it works almost as a parody of a parody. Batchelor embraced the challenge of the film, recognising the profound difficulty of reducing the opera by over half of its original length, while responding to the condition that no words or songs could be altered or rewritten. The story was hard to adapt because it contained numerous sub-plots, involving, for example 'Mad Margaret', and Robin's loyal retainer, and changes of identity in the main characters. For Batchelor, a strong story relied on a sympathetic lead character and appropriate expositional dialogue, but here again, the story was already embedded in the song, making it less accessible and harder to understand. This led Batchelor ultimately to employ voiceover to help with narrative clarity and continuity, and to emphasise the central role of Robin Oakapple. Crucially, though, the animation itself always worked in the service of the expression of the emotion in the music, and enhanced the narrative with close attention to the gestures and attitudes of the characters, especially, for example, when Robin metamorphoses back into Sir Ruthven. Batchelor herself admitted that the first half of the film took too long to establish character and situation, but little could be done to change this in the light of the conditions imposed on her.

Only in the second half of the film is there a genuine justification for animation in the more fantastical and supernatural episodes. The story had sixteen sequences, some with as many as 72 scenes, and relied a great deal on performance-orientated character animation. The D'Oyly Carte Opera Company, for all its prevarication and anxiety about the project, nevertheless saw the film as having cultural importance, particularly in reaching new audiences who may have not encountered Gilbert and Sullivan before.

Though it is well known that John Halas wrote prodigiously about animation in numerous books

A sketch for Mad Margaret (above) and Joy's instructions for the colour and style of the bridesmaids (right).

Joy working on the design with Ted Pettingell (left).

Ruddigore 1964

Ruddigore was intended as a 'cultural film'. The main trouble was that it was not the culture of the day and Gilbert and Sullivan were not in any position to update the words to make it acceptable to a different age and audience.

A take-off of a nineteenth century melodrama, the story concerns a luckless baronet who has inherited a witch's curse laid on his family in reprisal for being burnt. The story, complicated by many sub-plots, and by the change of identity of most of the main characters, was asking a lot of essentially a simple medium.

The first step was to edit it to size, and the next to decide what to keep, what to discard, and what to change in the way of action and locale, since one of the conditions of making the film was that no words of songs be altered or rewritten.

Transposing this two-hour comic opera into a one-hour animated television special involved a great deal of industry and a breakdown of the film into sixteen sequences, some with as many as 72 scenes.

A cartoon character, to succeed, has to remain in character. In addition, much of the story was song, which made it that more difficult to grasp. On film, and even more in television, there is only *now* to get the point across fully. More than half the film had to be devoted to establishing the characters and situations - far too long.

Joy Batchelor
Scriptwriting for Animation

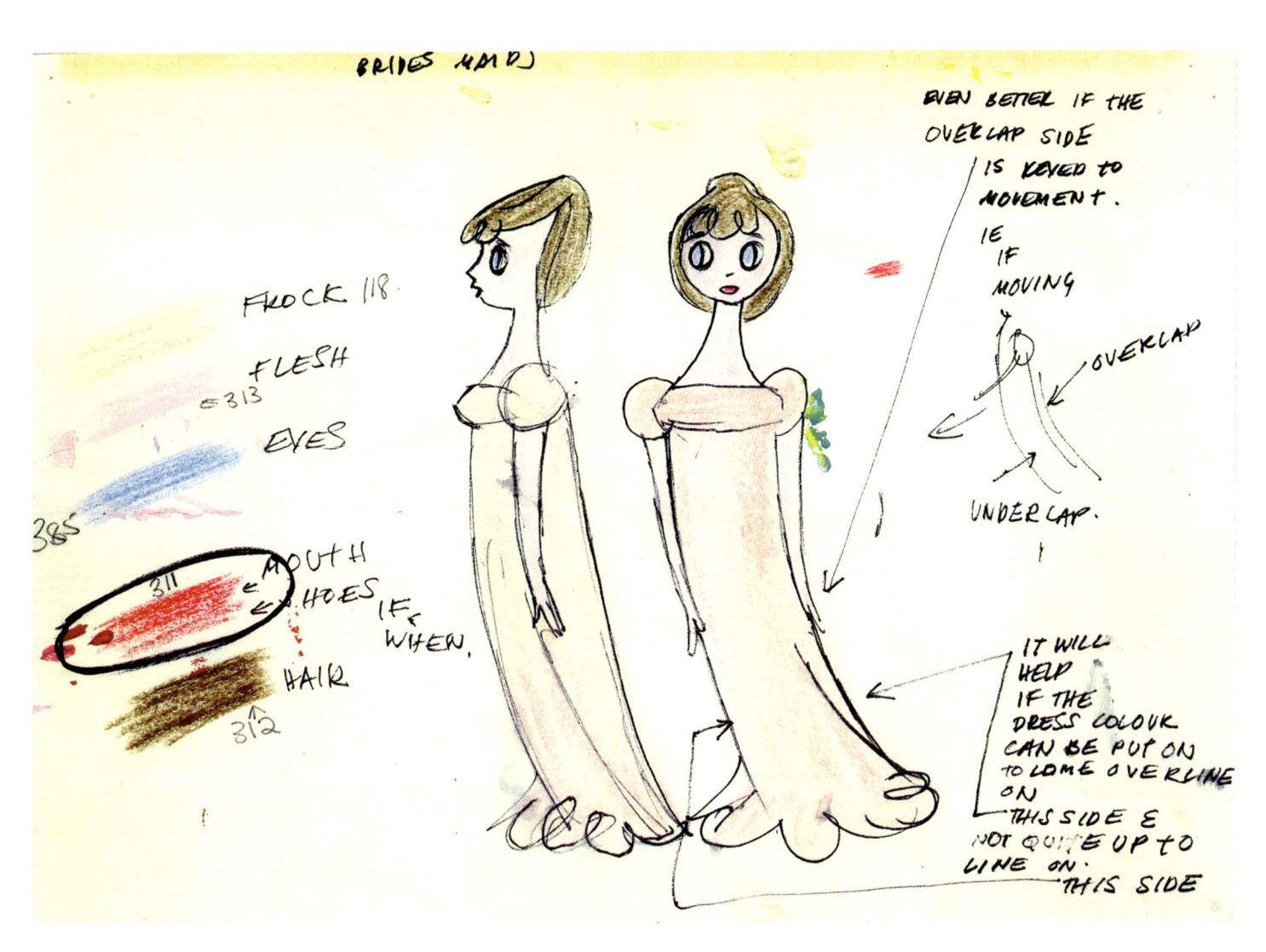

BRIDES MAID

FROCK 118
FLESH E313
EYES
385
MOUTH 311
SHOES IF & WHEN
HAIR 312

EVEN BETTER IF THE OVERLAP SIDE IS KEYED TO MOVEMENT. IE IF MOVING

OVERLAP

UNDERLAP.

IT WILL HELP IF THE DRESS COLOUR CAN BE PUT ON TO COME OVER LINE ON THIS SIDE & NOT QUITE UP TO LINE ON THIS SIDE

Modern Guide to Health (1946)

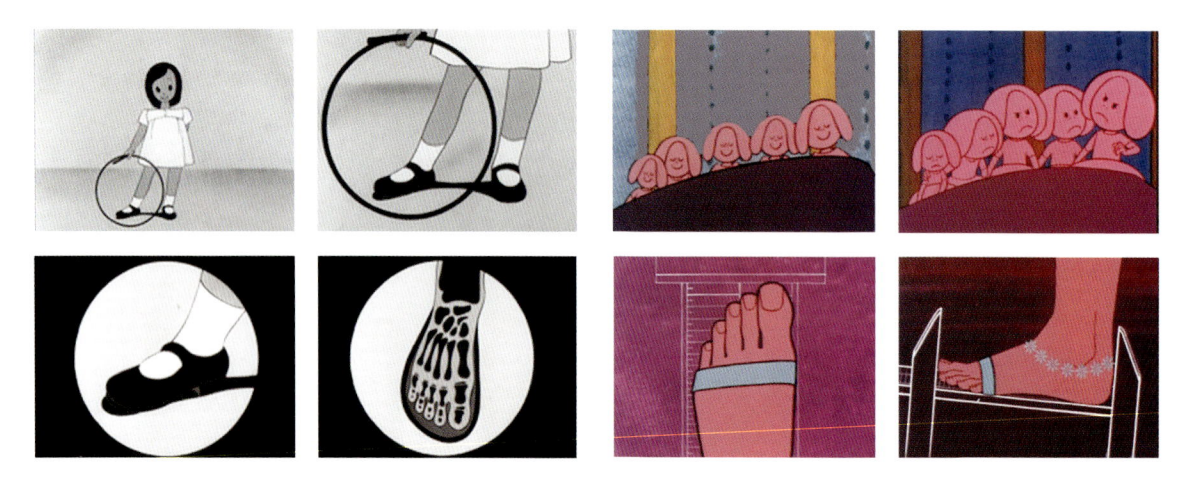

The Five (1970)

and articles, it is less acknowledged that Batchelor also theorised her approach, particularly during the late 1960s and the mid-1970s when she was an instrumental figure in Halas & Batchelor's Educational Film Centre. Papers in the Halas & Batchelor Collection reveal that Batchelor wrote talks and articles to explain her craft as a screenwriter working in the particular medium of animation, which she considered to have a specific 'language' of expression. Batchelor's constant preoccupation is how animation can be used pertinently within a British economy that is vastly different from the Hollywood model; how it should specifically address its audience; and interestingly, in a more implicitly evangelical way, how animation could, and perhaps, should be used to advance a greater recognition of the importance of visual literacy, and reduce the perennial engagement with language and text as the mediators of culture and society. Like Halas,

Batchelor believed that animation could be readily used in the service of social good, and another example of her work is instructive in this sense.

The Five (1970) is once more concerned with foot care for girls of eleven years and older. *Modern Guide to Health* (1946) used an authoritative, some might say, authoritarian voice to point out that wearing poorly fitting shoes will have future harmful consequences. By the late 1960s, though, after 'Swinging London', significant shifts in attitudes to sex, and the rise of Second Wave Feminism, the mode of address was different. There was a distinct and radical shift to a more pluralist agenda, and a sense that the claims to equality for women chimed also with a greater social desire for nonconformism and progressive notions of individuality. As Batchelor points out, 'Quite obviously the didactic approach was out. So was the voice of *authority*. The appeal to this particular audience had to be emotional and it is well nigh impossible to be emotional about a foot. There were other considerations to take into account. Young girls today buy shoes for fashion. This was intended as a long-life film, and as shoe shapes change yearly, showing shoes was *out*. Showing deformed feet was *out* for no young girl of twelve can be expected to identify herself with what she will become twenty or thirty years later, as a direct result of wearing badly fitting shoes *now*. Batchelor's solution was to personify the five toes of a young girl's foot as if they were five sisters. The girl returns home after a party and the toes bemoan how tired and sore they are. They relive the day, first as the girl goes to the shoe shop, but does not get a fitting, then as she goes through numerous boxes choosing new shoes. She walks home in the new shoes, and we feel the experience from the point of view of the toes, who suffer further at the disco the same evening, ending the night trodden on, and in pain. Finally relieved of the burden of the shoe, and settling to rest, the big toe dreams of the joys of a proper fitting and a shoe that affords the opportunity for the toes to have room and to grow straight.

Playful and entertaining, the film uses the particular capacity in animation for anthropomorphism to speak to its audience without patronising or offending them. The film invites empathy with the toes' predicament, and suggests an easy solution that does not operate prohibitively or critically to the target audience. Animating the toes as characters in their own right enables the issue to be addressed, cleverly bypassing the competing factors that might undermine or confuse the message.

This is a direct consequence of Batchelor's concentration on the role of the script and storyboarding in preproduction, both vehicles by which to identify the problems to be represented, to test the ways in which they can reach the proposed audience, and to extend the visual idioms that might apprehend the preoccupations - small scale and big picture - of the contemporary era.

One final, and singularly unsung project, *Contact* (1973), sponsored by the General Electric Company, is another exemplar of the ways in which animation can transcend space and time, here demonstrating the history and science in the advance of electricity. Batchelor was especially invested in the film, and believed it to be one of her most satisfying achievements. Combining classical storytelling scenarios in a serious and considered style, echoing the tone of works like *Animal Farm*, with the graphic idioms drawn from the instructional and utility film, *Contact* once again embodies Halas & Batchelor's commitment to both aesthetic and industrial modernism. Moving from the 'belle epoque' - the utopian period between the late 1870s and the outbreak of World War One (the first wave of Modernism epitomised by the building of the Eiffel Tower) - to the contemporary machinations of scientific and technological development in the early 1970s, the film is a tour de force of the principles of physics played out as both abstract aesthetics and a model of conceptual teaching and learning.

Batchelor is careful, though, to also show the interfaces between technological progress and the effect upon humankind, presenting simultaneously the art of the scientific principle, its technical execution, and its outcome and consequences. At the very same time as radical feminism was beginning to make its claims, Batchelor makes one of her most important films, speaking to those other preoccupations that bestrode her life - the growth of the mass media, and the development of new creative idioms. Though still unsung herself in many ways, Batchelor's vision permeates through the film in her joy that 'visual communication connects every corner of the globe', and that by maintaining a quasi-utopian belief in creative practice, both in art and science, that it was still possible to create 'a world full of life and optimism'.

Joy Batchelor is simply one of the most important British women film-makers, per se, and certainly, the most significant and influential British female animation director. Her body of films outweighs many far more acknowledged and celebrated figures, and includes work of the highest quality. Though she was marginalised by the vestiges of social and institutional sexism, and worked at a time that did not properly recognise her skills and achievements, it is clear that Batchelor can be readily reclaimed as a pioneer in modernist practices in the industrial and utility idioms of animated film; an exemplary screenwriter in all forms of animation, from the commercial to the feature; and as a visionary who not merely shared her husband's desire for utopian change, but grounded her efforts in the reality of training and education. This has benefited the many women now working in illustration, graphic design and animation in the contemporary era, and helped champion animation as the most dynamic exemplar of visual literacy and communication design.

Bibliography
Halas, V. & Wells, P. *Halas & Batchelor Cartoons: An Animated History* (London: Southbank Publishing, 2006).
Hediger, V. & Vonderau, P. (eds). *Films That Work: Industrial Film and the Productivity of Media* (Amsterdam: Amsterdam University Press, 2009).
See 'Dustbins and Defence: Halas and Batchelor and British Animation 1939-1949' in Thoms, D. & Kirkham, P. (eds). *War Culture* London: Lawrence and Wishart, 1995, pp. 61-72.
See *An Animated Utopia: The Life and Achievement of John Halas 1912-1995* (Dir: Wells, P., UK, 2012).

Note
When undertaking public lectures in the 1970s, having established the Educational Film Centre, Batchelor discovered that her work was called 'Communication Design' on college and university syllabi. She comments upon this ironically in her paper 'Educating Image Makers' (24/1/76), an unpublished piece from the Halas & Batchelor Collection.

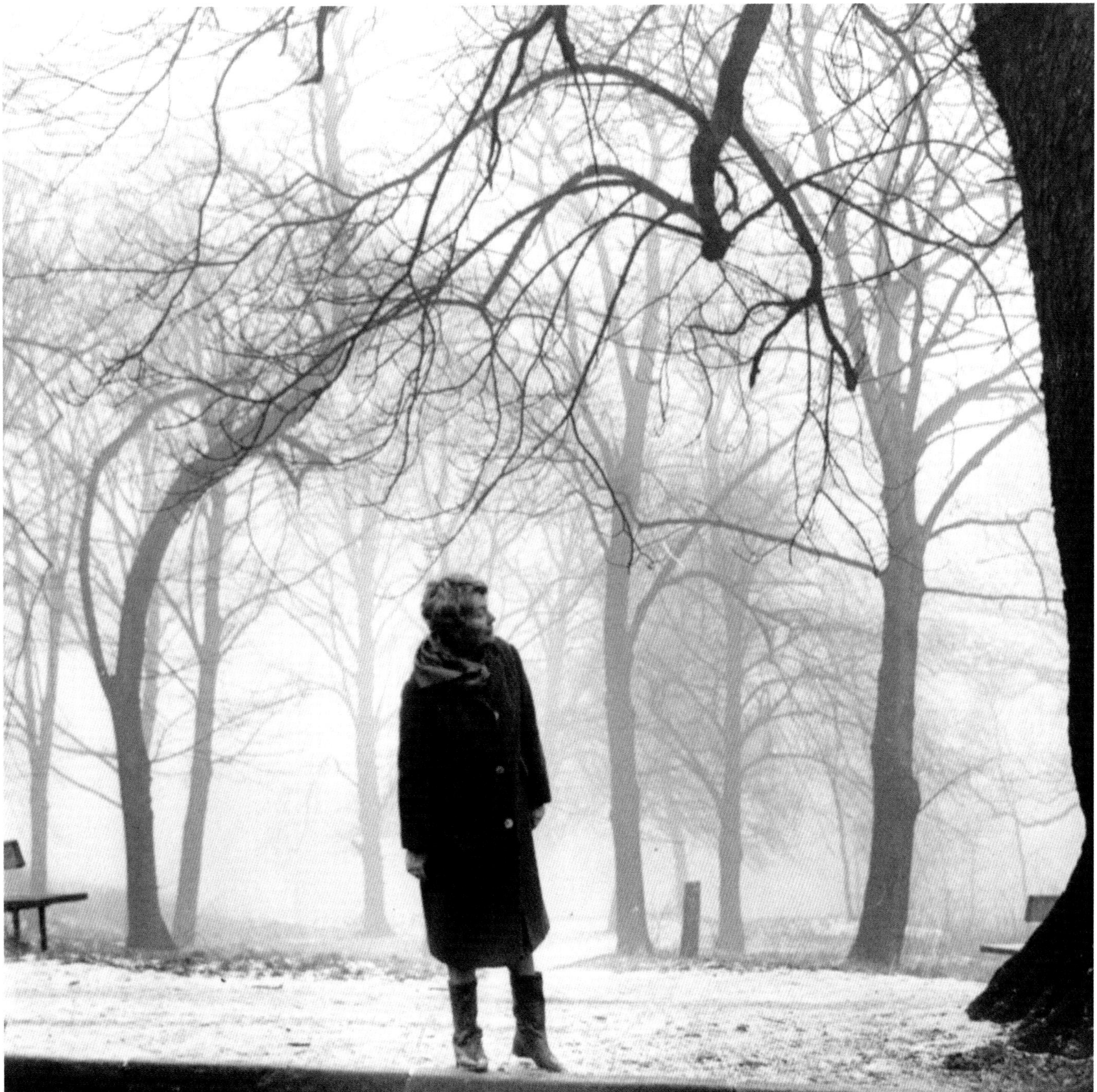

Filmography and films

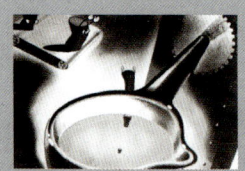

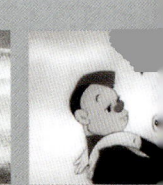

Film	Date	Company	Sponsor	Direction	Production	Script	Animation	Design
Robin Hood	1935	Champion	MGM	•			•	
Brave Tin Soldier	1938	British Colour Cartoons	BCC	•		•	•	•
Music Man	1938	British Colour Cartoons	BCC	•		•	•	
The Pocket Cartoon	1940	JWT Productions	MOI	•			•	
Carnival in the Clothes Cupboard	1940	JWT Productions	Lux	•	•	•	•	•
Dustbin Parade	1941	Realist Film Unit	MOI	•	•	•	•	
Filling the Gap	1941	Realist Film Unit	MOI	•	•	•	•	
Digging for Victory	1942	Realist Film Unit	MOI	•	•	•	•	•
Fable of the Fabrics	1942	JWT Productions	Lux	•	•	•	•	•
Compost Heaps	1943	Halas & Batchelor	MOI	•	•	•	•	
Model Sorter	1943	Halas & Batchelor	MOI	•	•	•	•	
I Stopped, I Looked	1943	Halas & Batchelor	MOI	•	•	•	•	
Compost Heaps	1943	Halas & Batchelor	MOI	•	•	•	•	
Early Digging	1943	Halas & Batchelor	MOI	•	•	•	•	
Jungle Warfare	1943	Halas & Batchelor	MOI	•	•			•
Abu series								
Abu's Harvest	1943	Halas & Batchelor	MOI	•	•			
Abu's Dungeon	1943	Halas & Batchelor	MOI	•	•			
Abu and the Poisoned Well	1944	Halas & Batchelor	MOI	•	•			
Abu Builds a Dam	1944	Halas & Batchelor	MOI	•	•			
Cold Comfort	1944	Halas & Batchelor	MOI	•	•	•	•	
From Rags to Stitches	1944	Halas & Batchelor	MOI	•	•	•	•	

Film	Date	Company	Sponsor	Direction	Production	Script	Animation	Design
Blitz on Bugs	1944	Halas & Batchelor	MOI	•	•	•	•	
Mrs Sew and Sew	1944	Halas & Batchelor	MOI	•	•	•	•	
Christmas Wishes	1944	Halas & Batchelor	MOI	•	•	•	•	
The Big Top	1944	Halas & Batchelor	MOI	•	•	•	•	
Tommy's Double Trouble	1944	Halas & Batchelor	MOI	•	•		•	
Six Little Jungle Boys	1945	JWT Productions	MOI	•	•		•	
Old Wives' Tales	1945	Halas & Batchelor	MOI	•	•	•		•
Good King Wenceslas	1945	Halas & Batchelor	MOI			•		
Modern Guide to Health	1946	Halas & Batchelor	MOI	•	•	•		•
Train Trouble	1946	Halas & Batchelor	Kelloggs	•	•		•	
Radio Ructions	1946	Halas & Batchelor	Kelloggs	•	•	•	•	
This is the Air Force	1946	Halas & Batchelor	MOI	•	•	•		
First Line of Defence	1946	Halas & Batchelor	MOI	•	•			
What's Cooking?	1947	Halas & Batchelor	Brook Bond	•	•	•		•
Dolly Put the Kettle On	1947	Halas & Batchelor	Brook Bond	•	•	•		•
Charley series								
Charley's March of Time	1948	Halas & Batchelor	COI	•	•	•		•
Charley in the New Towns	1948	Halas & Batchelor	COI	•	•	•		•
Robinson Charley	1948	Halas & Batchelor	COI	•	•	•		•
Charley's Black Magic	1948	Halas & Batchelor	COI	•	•	•		•
Farmer Charley	1949	Halas & Batchelor	COI	•	•	•		•
Charley Junior's Schooldays	1949	Halas & Batchelor	COI	•	•	•		•

Film	Date	Company	Sponsor	Direction	Production	Script	Animation	Design
Very Good Health	1949	Halas & Batchelor	COI					
Heave Away My Johnny	1948	Halas & Batchelor	GDF	•	•	•		
Oxo Parade	1948	Halas & Batchelor	OXO	•	•	•		
Magic Canvas	1948	Halas & Batchelor	H&B	•				
RAF - First Line of Defence	1949	Halas & Batchelor	COI	•	•			•
Water for Fire Fighting	1949	Halas & Batchelor	Home Office		•			•
Fly about the House	1949	Halas & Batchelor	COI	•	•	•		•
The Shoemaker and the Hatter	1949	Halas & Batchelor	EEC	•	•	•		•
British Army at Your Service	1950	Halas & Batchelor	COI	•	•			
We've Come a Long Way	1951	Halas & Batchelor	BP			•		
Flu-ing Squad	1951	Halas & Batchelor	Aspro	•	•			
The Figurehead	1953	Halas & Batchelor	H&B	•	•	•		•
Moving Spirit	1953	Halas & Batchelor	BP	•				
The Owl and the Pussycat	1953	Halas & Batchelor	H&B	•				
Down a Long Way	1954	Halas & Batchelor	BP			•		
Animal Farm	1954	Halas & Batchelor	DeRochemont	•	•	•		•
Power to Fly	1954	Halas & Batchelor	BP			•		
Refinery at Work	1955	Halas & Batchelor	BP			•		
Cinerama Holiday	1955	Cinerama	DeRochemont					★
To Your Health	1956	Halas & Batchelor	WHO		•			
Think of the Future	1956	Halas & Batchelor	EEC		•			
History of the Cinema	1956	Halas & Batchelor	H&B		•			

★ Art direction

Film	Date	Company	Sponsor	Direction	Production	Script	Animation	Design
The World of Little Ig	1956	Halas & Batchelor	H&B/BBC		•	•		
Midsummer Nightmare	1957	Halas & Batchelor	H&B		•	•		
Animal, Vegetable, Mineral	1955	Halas & Batchelor	BP			•		
All Lit Up	1957	Halas & Batchelor	Gas Council	•	•	•		
The Candlemaker	1957	Halas & Batchelor	Lutheren[1]		•	•		
The Christmas Visitor	1958	Halas & Batchelor	H&B		•	•		
Dam the Delta	1958	Halas & Batchelor	NIS	•		•		
Speed to the Plough	1958	Halas & Batchelor	BP			•		
How to be a Hostess	1958	Halas & Batchelor	Lintas★			•		
Follow That Car	1958	Halas & Batchelor	Shell		•			
Paying Bay	1958	Halas & Batchelor	Shell			•		
Piping Hot	1959	Halas & Batchelor	BP	•	•	•		
Energy Picture	1959	Halas & Batchelor	BP			•		
For Better, For Worse	1961	Halas & Batchelor	Philips		•	•		
Hamilton in the Music Festival	1961	Halas & Batchelor	H&B		•	•		
Hamilton the Musical Elephant	1961	Halas & Batchelor	H&B		•	•		
The Monster of Highgate Ponds	1961	H&B / Children's Film Foundation★				•		
Monsieur Carre's Adventure	1962	Halas & Batchelor	Macmillan			•		
Automania 2000	1963	Halas & Batchelor	H&B			•		
Ruddigore	1964	Halas & Batchelor	H&B/WBC[2]	•	•	•		•
Follow That Car	1964	Halas & Batchelor			•	•		
Paying Bay	1964	Halas & Batchelor			•	•		

[1] Lutheren Church Federation of the USA
[2] WBC New York
★ Live action & stop motion

Film	Date	Company	Sponsor	Direction	Production	Script	Animation	Design
Dying for a Smoke	1966	Halas & Batchelor	COI			•		
Classic Fairy Tales								
The Frog Prince	1966	Halas & Batchelor	EB[1]	•		•		
Rumpelstiltzkin	1966	Halas & Batchelor	EB	•		•		
Hansel and Gretel	1967	Halas & Batchelor	EB	•		•		
The Sleeping Beauty	1967	Halas & Batchelor	EB	•		•		
The Ugly Ducking	1967	Halas & Batchelor	EB	•		•		
Little Tom Thumb	1967	Halas & Batchelor	EB	•		•		
The Columbo Plan	1967	Halas & Batchelor	COI	•	•	•		
The Commonwealth	1967	Halas & Batchelor	COI	•	•	•		
Flurina	1968	Halas & Batchelor	Condor			•		
Bolly in a Space Adventure	1968	Halas & Batchelor	H&B	•	•	•		
Children and Cars	1970	Halas & Batchelor	BP		•	•		
The Five	1970	Halas & Batchelor	BMA	•	•	•		
Wotdot	1970	Halas & Batchelor	H&B	•	•	•		•
Children Making Cartoons	1973	Educational Film Centre			•	•		
Contact	1973	Educational Film Centre	CGE[2]	•		•		
Carry on Milkmaids	1973	Educational Film Centre	SMM[3]	•	•	•		
European Folk Tales								
The Ass and the Stick	1974	Educational Film Centre	Corona Rome	•				
Christmas Feast	1974	Educational Film Centre	Corona Rome	•				

The dates given are either the production or release dates of the films.

[1] Encyclopedia Britannica
[2] Compagne Générale d'Electricité Paris
[3] Scottish Milk Marketing

Film selection

Background from *The Shoemaker and the Hatter* (1949).

Dustbin Parade 1941

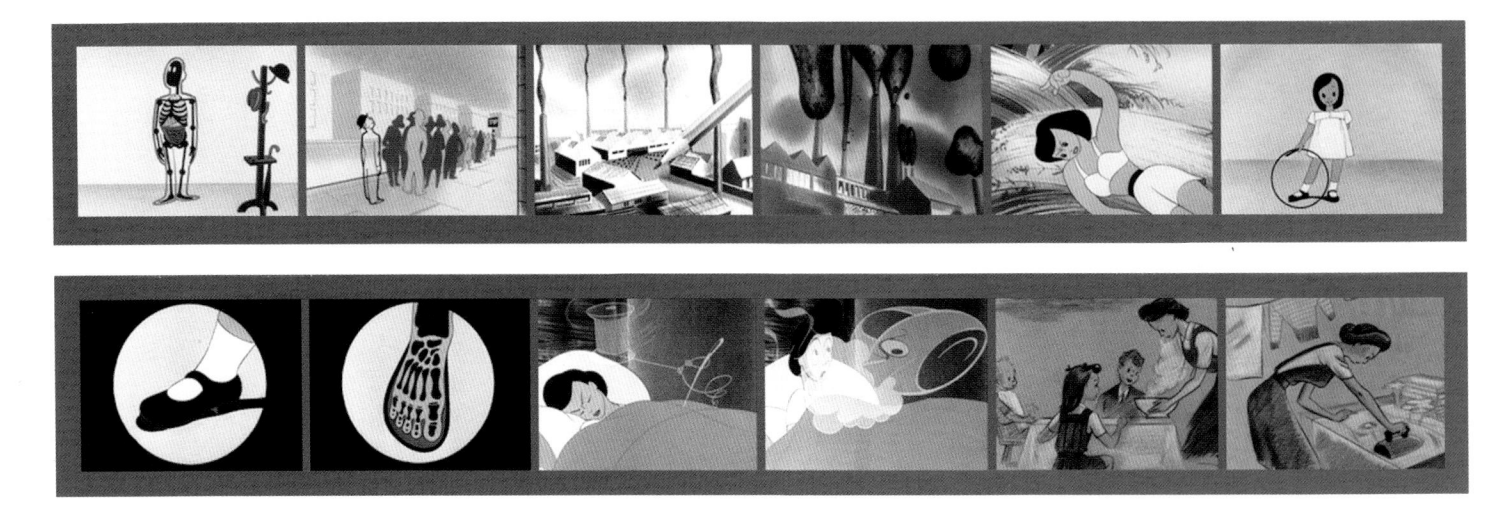

Modern Guide to Health 1946

Radio Ructions 1946

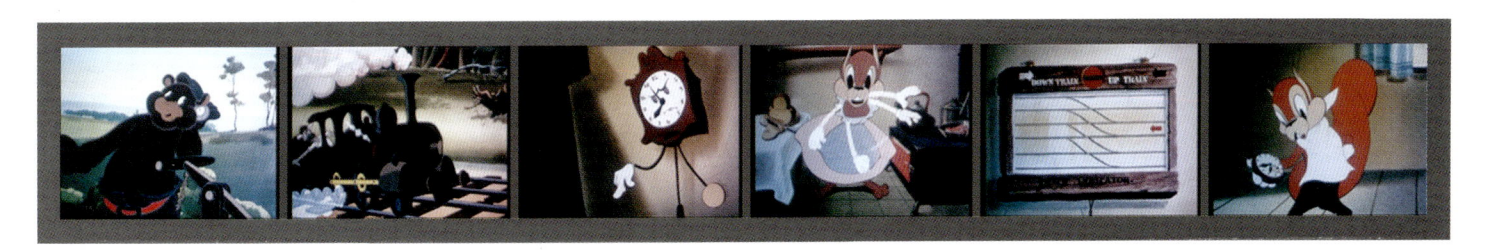

Train Trouble 1946

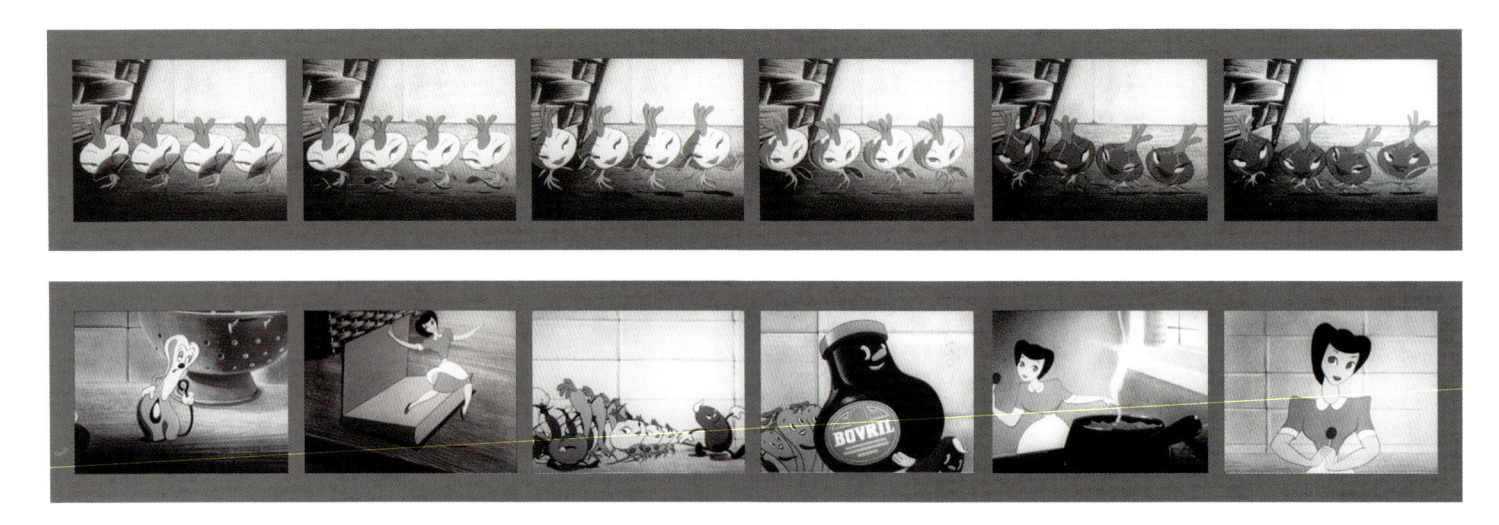

What's Cooking? 1947

Dolly Put the Kettle On 1947

Charley in the New Towns 1948

The Shoemaker and the Hatter 1949

The Figurehead 1953

Animal Farm 1954

90

All Lit Up 1957

Piping Hot 1959

Automania 2000 1963

Ruddigore 1964

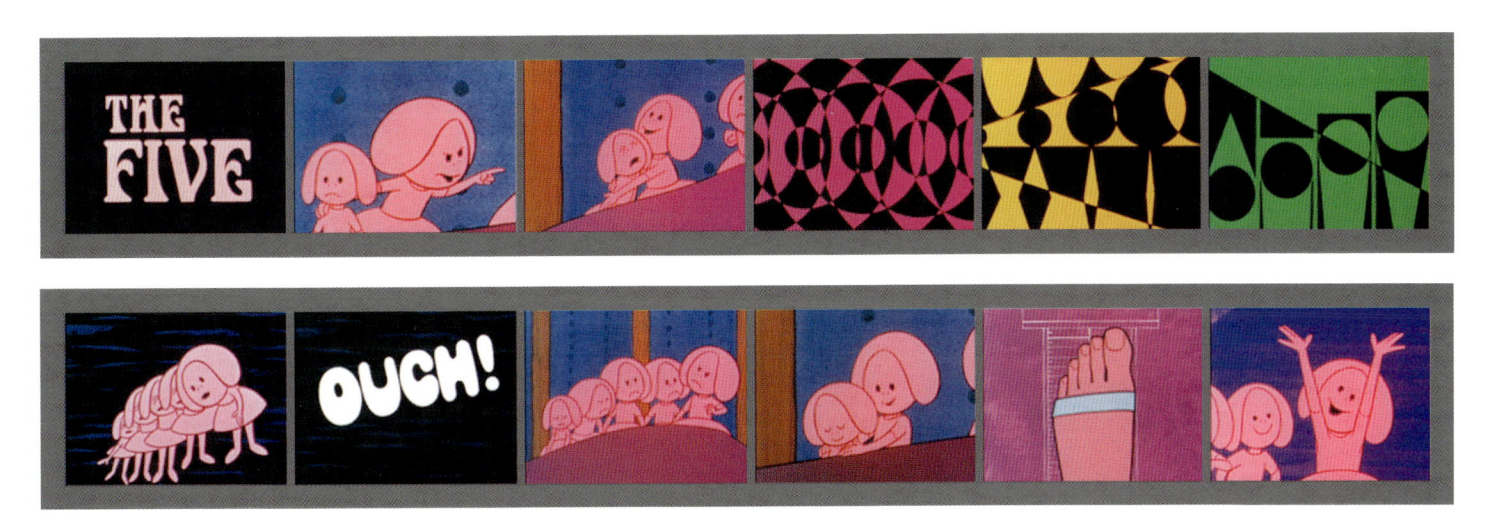

The Five 1970

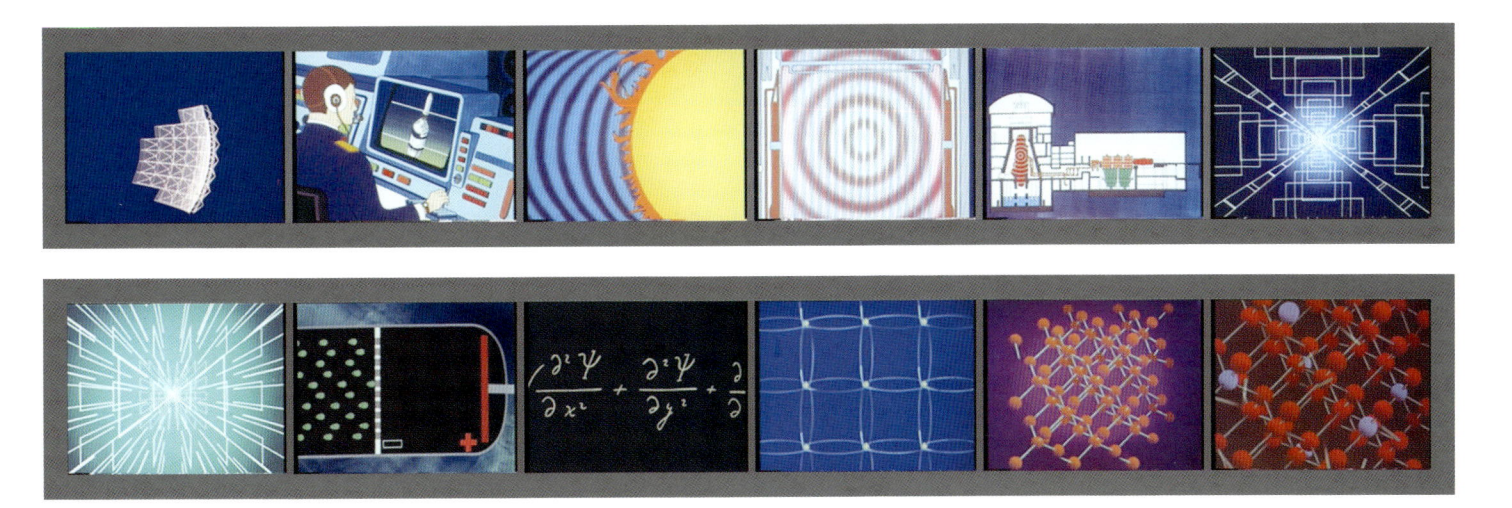

Contact 1973

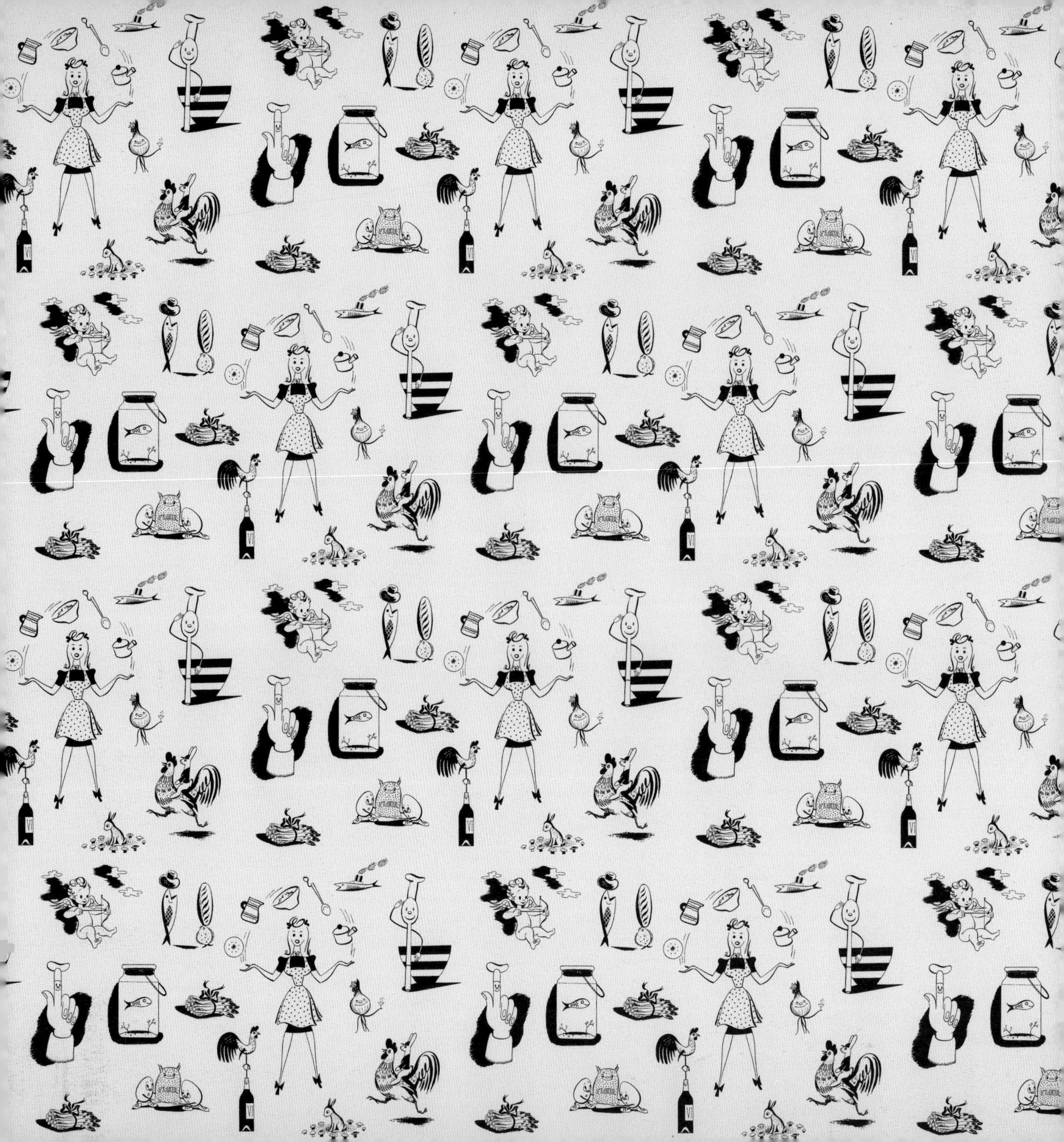